# Wisconsin

## OFF THE BEATEN PATH™

"Martin Hintz fills in the miles with meaning and flavor."
—Gary Knowles, former director of the bureau of
communications, Wisconsin Tourism Development

"Most travel guides give only cursory attention to Wisconsin;
it's necessary to have a specialty title such as this to gain the
most from a visit to the state."
—*Midwest Book Review*

OFF THE BEATEN PATH SERIES

# Wisconsin

## OFF THE BEATEN PATH™

### THIRD EDITION

## MARTIN AND DAN HINTZ

*A Voyager Book*

The Globe Pequot Press

Old Saybrook, Connecticut

Illustrations by Carole Drong
Cover map copyright © DeLorme Mapping

Off the Beaten Path is a trademark of The Globe Pequot Press, Inc.

**Library of Congress Cataloging-in-Publication Data**
Hintz, Martin.
  Winsconsin : off the beaten path / by Martin and Dan Hintz.—3rd ed.
    p. cm.  — (Off the beaten path series)
  Includes index.
  ISBN 1-56440-730-6
  1. Wisconsin—Guidebeooks. I. Hintz, Dan.  II. Title.  III. Series
F379.3.H56  1995
917.7504'43—dc20                                         95-19280
                                                          CIP


Manufactured in the United States of America
Third Edition/Third Printing

*To the family, travelers all*

NORTHERN

CENTRAL

EASTERN

WESTERN

MILWAUKEE

**WISCONSIN**

# CONTENTS

# Acknowledgments

Special gratitude to all our friends throughout Wisconsin who helped with this book, especially Gary Knowles, Ronda Allen, and the staff of the Wisconsin Division of Tourism. Visitor bureaus, historical societies, and local information offices around the state were particularly helpful as well. The people of Wisconsin themselves also deserve a rousing hand clap: from the guy who told us where to find the best pie in his hometown to the volunteer at the local historical site. Thanks.

# INTRODUCTION

Wisconsin is a state of imagery: cows, woods, beer, fish.

Sure enough.

But the state has a lot more to offer. For instance, think of Wisconsin in superlatives: It has the world's largest four-sided clock, the biggest penny, and most massive loon. It offers a giant, five-story leaping muskie in whose massive mouth avid fisherfolk can even be married. The state cradles the nation's most comprehensive collection of works by beloved graphic artist Norman Rockwell and the world's finest assemblage of Haitian primitive paintings. The country's only whooping crane preserve is in Wisconsin, and so is a record-sized black bear. The cranes are alive and flopping. The bear is stuffed.

Wisconsin is a place for doing and seeing. It hosts the country's annual (shiver!) snow sculpting championships and the grandest old-time circus parade (hold yer hosses!) that ever graced any community's streets.

There are lead mines, cornfields, and superconductors. There are ship manufacturers, goats on top of restaurants, and milk carton raft races. One city boasts of its own submarine; another hosts the world's busiest airstrip during a summertime fly-in of experimental and private aircraft.

Wisconsin is a state tailor-made for off-the-beaten-path adventures. You can discover some of the secrets in a corridor of Madison's stately Capitol Building, on the rocky tip of foggy Door County, in a pine-scented North Woods glade, on a narrow Milwaukee side street.

*Wisconsin: Off the Beaten Path* ranges from urban to rural and back again. Dan and I hope that this book will lighten your travel planning, heighten your sensibilities, and increase your fun.

The enthusiastic explorer can use this poke-along guide to uncover secluded hideaways, as well to discover hints about getting around the more well known tourist attractions.

Care has been taken to ensure accuracy as much as possible. Over time, however, ticket prices, phone numbers, and hours of operation may change; establishments may close for one reason or another; and personnel may move on. Subsequently, there may be a few discrepancies in this edition that will have to wait for the next updating of *Wisconsin*. So please be patient and let the publisher know of any necessary adjustments, because you, as reader, can also be a great scout. Who knows what neat new Wisconsin discoveries you will find to share with other readers!

Costs for meals, lodgings, and attractions are remarkably reasonable in Wisconsin. The ratings we gave for meals are $2.50 to $6.00 low, $7.00 to $12 moderate, and $13 and above high. For rooms, $16 to $30 is low, $31 to $55 is moderate, and $56 and up is expensive. Attraction prices are low if they are between $2.00 and $3.50; moderate, $4.00 to $6.00; and high, $7.00 and above. Of course, each price has many variables, depending on length of show, type of attraction, and so on. The prices and rates listed in this guidebook were accurate at press time. We recommend, however, that you call establishments before traveling in order to get the most up-to-date information.

On your journeys, always, always remember to verify lodging arrangements before arrival. It pays to call ahead. Even that most off-the-beaten-path bed and breakfast could be booked the night you wish to register.

Resident admission stickers for Wisconsin state parks cost $15.00 annually, $4.00 daily, and $2.00 for one hour. For resident senior citizens (sixty-five and older), stickers are $6.50 annually and $2.00 daily. For nonresidents, the cost is $24.00 annually, $6.00 daily, and $2.00 for one hour. Stickers are required on all motor vehicles entering and stopping in state parks. They can be purchased at the parks, at local Department of Natural Resources (DNR) offices, or by writing the DNR, Bureau of Parks and Recreation, Box 7921, Madison 53707 (608–266–2181). Half-price annual tickets are available for additional vehicles in a family.

Although half the fun is in getting here, you may need some time-fillers for the tykes in the back seat. So here are some background statistics and little details to use when, for the umpteenth time, the youngsters ask if they are having fun yet. Have them guess these facts:

Population of Wisconsin: 4.8 million
State tree: maple
State bird: robin
State animal: badger
State fish: muskie
State capital: Madison
State cheese: Colby
Length of Wisconsin: 300 miles

Width of Wisconsin: 280 miles
Annual average snowfall: 45 inches
Forest area: 14,487,000 acres
Lakes: 14,927 (largest is Lake Winnebago at 137,708 acres)
Golf courses: 369
Bike trails: 10,000 miles
Off-road bike trails: 155 miles
Camping sites: 51,748
Cross-country skiing: 20,835 miles
State-operated snowmobile trails: 94 (10,000 miles)
State parks: 60
Had enough?

Aw, how about a few more for the record? Wisconsin has 500 different types of soils; 108,000 miles of roads; 2,444 fantastic trout streams and a couple that aren't so good (those are the ones where we don't bag our limit); the Fox River flows north (one of the few in the country to do so); and Beatles recording luminary Paul McCartney owns the rights to the rousing state song, "On Wisconsin."

That doesn't faze Wisconsinites, who put a slogan on everything else. Most crossroads have some sort of booster phrase that proudly adorns signage leading to Main Street. You can take a plunge in Amery, "City of Lakes"; pedal like crazy in Brodhead, "The Bicycle Gateway to Wisconsin"; shake hands in Cumberland, "Famous for Friendliness"; move ahead in Edgar, "A Progressive Village Serving People"; cover up in Cambridge, "The Umbrella City"; and have a "dam" lot of fun in Beaver Dam, "Home of 15,000 Busy Beavers."

You'll have to come to the state to find who is "Tops in Wisconsin," "The Gem City," and "Home of the World's Largest Sauerkraut Plant."

Wisconsin is also the capital of self-proclaimed "capitals." Almost every community worth its civic salt has given itself some municipal distinction. Onalaska is the Sunfish Capital. Birchwood is the Bluegill Capital. Algoma is the Trout and Salmon Capital. Bayfield is the Lake Trout Capital. And a fierce battle to retain the Walleye Capital tag is constantly being waged by Presque Isle, Stone Lake, and Long Lake (depends on the size and amount of the annual sport fishing catch, and, by the way, it takes an average of one hundred hours to catch a 33.4-inch muskie). With all these titles, don't think that there's something fishy about Wisconsin.

After all, Sheboygan is the Bratwurst Capital. Racine is the Kringle Capital. Green Bay is the Toilet Paper Capital (because of its paper products industry). Bloomer is the Rope Jumping Capital. Monroe is the Swiss Cheese Capital. Elmwood and Belleville each claim to be the UFO Capital of the World.

Consequently, it's quite obvious that visiting Wisconsin is a "capital" idea whether we're on or off the beaten path. But much of the fun in Wisconsin comes in discovery, in finding the little known and the really unexpected. You can find that out for yourself.

---

*The prices and rates listed in this guidebook were confirmed at press time. We recommend, however, that you call establishments before traveling to obtain current information.*

---

# WESTERN WISCONSIN

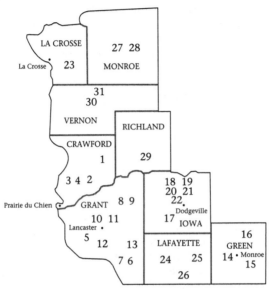

1. Blossom Day Festival
2. Kickapoo Indian Caverns
3. Villa Louis
4. Fort Crawford Medical Museum
5. Nelson Dewey State Park
6. Stonefield Village
7. Eagle Valley Nature Preserve
8. Grand Army of the Republic Hall
9. Spurgeon Vineyards and Winery
10. Fennimore Cheese Factory
11. Fennimore Doll Museum
12. Grant County Courthouse
13. Platteville Mining Museum
14. Jos. Huber Brewing Company
15. Sugar River Trail
16. Swiss historical village
17. Pendarvis
18. Folklore Village
19. FantaSuite Don Q Resort
20. Hillside Home School
21. American Players Theater
22. Springs Golf Club Resort
23. Riverside USA
24. First Capitol State Park and Museum
25. Blackhawk Memorial County Park
26. Badger Mine Museum
27. Elroy-Sparta Trail
28. Fiberglass Animals, Shapes and Trademarks
29. High School Rodeo Association Championships
30. Westby House
31. Norskedalen

# WESTERN WISCONSIN

The rolling, muddy waters of the Mississippi form most of the western boundary of Wisconsin. The river edges a slow way from where it first touches the state at Prescott, meandering 200 miles south to the rural southwestern corner of the state near Dubuque, Iowa. The Great River Road, Highway 35, skirts the rim of the river, crawling through sloughs, up over the ridgebacks, along short straightaways that end much too soon in a sweeping curve. The road has consistently been voted one of the country's most scenic routes by everyone from motorcycle clubs to travel editors. The route is well marked by white signs with a green riverboat pilot's wheel.

For a map of the entire Great River Road, covering the 3,000 miles from Canada to the Gulf of Mexico, contact the Mississippi River Parkway Commission, 336 Robert Street, St. Paul, MN 55101 (612–224–9903).

Muscular tugboats, with their roaring diesel engines, shove blocks of barges loaded with coal, oil, lumber, and other goods. They make these runs almost year-round between Minnesota's Twin Cities, Minneapolis and St. Paul, to the Gulf of Mexico. Only the freezing cold of midwinter forces closing of the river traffic. The river is then turned over to hardy anglers who brave the blustery winds in search of the Midwest's best-tasting bluegills and catfish. The hapless fish are plucked through holes chopped in ice that can be two or more feet thick.

Trappers range along the riverbanks, bringing in dozens of muskrat, beaver, and fox pelts each year to satisfy the demands of the national and international markets.

Passengers get rides straight out of Mark Twain days on riverboats such as the steam-spitting *Delta Queen* and her sisters that still ply the waters. The vessels call at quays in Prairie du Chien and La Crosse. The boats' appearances are often surprising. I remember camping on a riverfront sandbar one summer and being awakened in the predawn hours to the crash of paddle wheels storming downriver. A quick glance out the tent flap revealed what seemed to be a sky-high bank of lights surging south on the blackness of the river. Waltz music wafted through the humid night air, just audible over the roar of machinery. Then it was gone, like a nineteenth-century dream.

The river is dotted with islands, fringed with marshlands, and speckled with drowned trees, which are the reminders of the Mississippi's many spring run-off tantrums. But on decent days, canoeists can paddle along the backwater sloughs in search of great, flopping heron and slithery muskrats. Houseboaters can drift along in tune with seasons.

## CRAWFORD COUNTY

This is a county of rivers. The Wisconsin bisects the landscape, meandering downstream from the state's northlands. Its importance in history is marked by a sign in Portage (Columbia County) that reads: "On June 14, 1673, Jacques Marquette and Louis Joliet started the 1.28 mile portage from here to the Wisconsin River, which led to their discovery of the Upper Mississippi June 17, 1673, at Prairie du Chien."

Other markers in the county should be perused as well. While you are in Gays Mills for the annual ◈**Blossom Day Festival** in May, read the marker on Highway 171 east of town. It tells of the early lives of the pioneers who developed the apple industry there. A marker commemorating early Governor James Davidson is on Highway 61 near the village of Soldiers Grove. A marker on Highway 35 south of Lynxville describes the log rafts that used to float down the Mississippi in the 1800s. The Prairie du Chien marker is at the tourist information center on the Mississippi River, memorializing the building of the third frontier fort in the Wisconsin Territory. Another marker in Prairie du Chien, located at Villa Louis, outlines the importance of Fort Crawford in protecting the American frontier during the War of 1812. A Marquette-Joliet marker at the state's tourism information center where Highway 18 crosses the Mississippi honors the two French explorers and their five French-Canadian *voyageur* companions as being the first whites to travel the Upper Mississippi.

After the Mississippi and the Wisconsin, Crawford County's third major waterway is the Kickapoo, a name derived from the Winnebago Indian term *kwigapawa,* which means "moves about from here to there." The Winnebagos knew what they were talking about.

The Kickapoo offers more twists and turns than a dish of spaghetti on its crooked north and south route, joining the Wisconsin River at Wauzeka.

3

On Highway 60, just before entering Wauzeka from the west, are the ❖**Kickapoo Indian Caverns,** discovered by lead miners in the early 1800s. The caves are the state's largest, once used by local Indians as a shelter. Forty-minute guided tours can be taken through the caverns, formed by an underground river. Be sure to wear comfortable walking shoes and a sweater or jacket. The caverns are open from 9:00 A.M. to 4:15 P.M. daily from May 15 to October 31. For details on the rock formations, contact the Kickapoo Indian Caverns in Wauzeka at (608) 875–7723.

Lovely as it is, the Kickapoo can be nasty. The angry river waters flooded so often that the town of Soldiers Grove moved from its base along the cliffs to high ground in 1978. Originally called Pine Grove, the town of 680 was an encampment for troops during the Black Hawk War in 1832 and subsequently changed its name in honor of the soldiers.

All buildings in the rebuilt community, now high above the floodline, receive 50 percent or more of their power supply from the sun. The solar panels over the bank, supermarkets, clinic, stores, and homes give the town a futuristic look. The site of the former village has been turned into a riverside park with a ball diamond, campground, tennis courts, and picnic spot. Tourist information is available at the Solar Town Pharmacy, Box 95, Passive Sun Drive (608–624–3257).

The Old Oak Grove Inn in Soldiers Grove offers comfortable accommodations, a heated pool, and a restaurant that has some of the best sage-stuffed chicken in western Wisconsin. Room rates range from $36 to $62, with meals in the $4.50 to $14.50 spread.

Nearby is the Country Garden Restaurant, which offers, as the counter girl says, "great home cookin'." The Country Garden is usually just open for weekday lunches from 11:00 A.M. to 1:00 P.M., but it does have an all-you-can-eat fish fry on Friday evenings.

There are two explanations of how Prairie du Chien was named. One legend says the place was called "Field of the Dogs" by French trappers who gathered here and saw acres of prairie dog mounds. Another version says the town was named after "Big Dog," a local tribal leader. Whatever the real story, the city that evolved from the early frontier encampments has been a major Wisconsin trading center and river port for generations. Wisconsin's first millionaire, fur dealer Hercules Dousman, put the place on the map when he built his mansion ❖**Villa Louis** in 1843. That original house was razed in 1870, and the current Italianate building was constructed. The richly appointed building and its grounds are now owned by the State Historical Society of Wisconsin.

The Villa Louis, 521 Villa Louis Road (608–326–2721), is open from 9:00 A.M. to 5:00 P.M. daily May through October. Admission is $5.00 for adults and $2.00 for children. The family rate is $14. To get to the Villa from downtown Prairie, take Main Street north to Washington Street West.

There's a bit of personal history attached to the Villa Louis. My maternal great-grandmother, Bridget O'Malley, was a linen maid there when she came from Ireland to the United States around the time of the Civil War.

Her beau, Louie Larson, was a young Norwegian shopkeeper who lived in Marquette, on the Iowa side of the Mississippi. In the winter, Louie would ice skate across the river to court Bridget.

In the summer, he would take his sailboat *The Bluebird* across the river to pitch woo to his lady love. Naturally, Bridget was quite smitten with all this attention, and the couple eventually married and moved to Iowa. Viola! Without them, *Wisconsin: Off the Beaten Path* might never have been written—at least not by yours truly.

Great-grandma Bridget was always hospitable, according to reliable family memories, so she probably wouldn't mind the guests who come to the Villa each June to try their hand at preparing breakfast in a Victorian kitchen. Up to sixteen adults can sign up for a hands-on cooking class in the mansion's kitchen. Reservations are required; call the historic site. But as Bridget would have admonished, "Just clean up after yourselves and put everything back in the proper drawer."

Prairie also played another part in my family history. Great-uncle Charlie (one of the sons of the aforementioned Louie and Bridget) and a couple of his friends sneaked across the old railroad pontoon bridge that linked Iowa and Wisconsin at the turn of the century. They had hitched an all-night ride on an eastbound freight train from their hometown to see the Buffalo Bill Wild West Show in Prairie du Chien. They got more than their money's worth in that hot summer of 1901.

The showfolk and the townspeople began brawling in the streets, a brouhaha that resulted in calling out the Wisconsin militia. Uncle Charlie and his frightened young pals hid in an old boiler next to a tavern as they watched the boisterous "Hey, Rube!" That's circus slang for "a fight" between towners and circus workers. Buffalo Bill managed to round up his crew before the militia arrived and scurried westward across the river to the safety of Iowa.

It's a lot quieter now in Prairie du Chien. Down the street from the Villa Louis is the **St. Feriole Railroad Bar,** a tavern in an old railroad passenger car that claims to serve the best Bloody Marys on the Mississippi River.

Judge for yourself at 119 Water Street (608–326–4941). If you need to use the facilities, a tank car serves as a rest room. Other railroad cars on the siding at **St. Feriole Island** house the Gift Box and a dangerously delightful place called Confection Connection. The latter's homemade fudge is guaranteed to add happy tonnage to hips. The cars, however, are open only from May through October.

The island is actually a spit of land jutting into the Mississippi on the west side of the city. The cars are parked south of the quay used by the riverboat *Delta Queen* when it docks in **Lawler Park.** The site is at the end of Blackhawk Avenue, where the railroad pontoon bridge used to link Wisconsin to Iowa.

Each Father's Day, a rendezvous that brings alive memories of the fur trapper days is held on St. Feriole Island. Hundreds of reenactors portray traders, voyageurs, soldiers, and Native Americans in a large encampment of tents and huts. Interested in a skunk pelt? Tomahawk? Flintlock? Everything a frontier family could use is for sale. Even a contemporary suburban home can probably do with an iron kettle or two. There are black powder musket firings, dances, fiddling, tall tales, and plenty of rough-and-ready types to photograph. In mid-July, a War of 1812 military reenactment is held featuring British-Canadian and U.S. troops. The pageant is held on the lawn of the Villa Louis.

While in Prairie, stop at the ◆ **Fort Crawford Medical Museum,** 717 S. Beaumont Road (608–326–6960), and view its extensive collection of frontier surgical instruments and medical devices. Seen in today's light, they look more like inquisitor's tools than anything else. Dr. William Beaumont, whose studies on the digestive system revolutionized the medical world, was once stationed at Fort Crawford. While there, he conducted some of his experiments on a French-Canadian trapper who had been wounded in the stomach. Beaumont would put food, tied onto a string, into the man's stomach and withdraw it for study. The doctor published a book about his experiences in 1853.

The fort, built by Zachary Taylor and Jefferson Davis, was one of the most important outposts in the young United States, especially during the Black Hawk Indian War. Hours are 10:00 A.M. to 5:00 P.M., May through Halloween. Admission is $2.50; $1.00 for children six to twelve; five and under free; and a $6.00 family rate.

## GRANT COUNTY

Grant County is tucked into the far southwestern corner of Wisconsin, where the Mississippi joins the state with Iowa and Illinois. The county has some 49 miles of prime river frontage on its western border and 42 miles of Wisconsin River on its northern rim. To capitalize on this watery connection, the county operates ten boat landings on the rivers, augmenting the dozens of private put-in sites.

The landscape consists of rolling ridges and deep valleys, with thick stands of oak and maple trees overlooking the water ways. ◆**Nelson Dewey State Park** and **Wyalusing State Park** offer the best scenic overviews. Each perches some 400 to 500 feet on the limestone crests towering above the valley floors. Excellent views of the confluence of the Wisconsin and the Mississippi can be had at Wyalusing on Highway X near Bagley.

In addition to bird-watching possibilities, Nelson Dewey State Park (named after Wisconsin's first governor) near Cassville offers a good view of the ◆**Stonefield Village** historic site (608–725–5210). Take County Trunk Road VV north of town to the Village (across the highway from the entrance to the state park), operated by the state historical society.

The community is a re-creation of an 1890s village, complete with railroad station, shops, firehouse, and school. The facility is open from 9:00 A.M. to 5:00 P.M. daily from Memorial Day through the first week in October. Stonefield is a good place to bring kids, who can talk with costumed interpreters portraying characters of the period.

A moody color photo of Stonefield, taken from the Nelson Dewey bluffs just as the morning fog was shredded by the oaks, captured the grand prize in a Wisconsin tourism division photo contest. Needless to say, the place is photogenic . . . with or without the mist. So bring cameras and plenty of color and black-and-white film.

7

**Stonefield Village**

Six miles north of Stonefield on Highway VV is the ❖ **Eagle Valley Nature Preserve,** called one of the world's best vantage points for watching migrating bald eagles. The preserve covers 1,440 acres, located 10 miles north of Cassville. The best times for viewing are from January to mid-March and from mid-September to mid-October. For information about the nonprofit preserve, contact Manager Bret Mandernacic, Duncan Road, Glen Haven 53810 (608–794–2373). Donations are accepted for the operation of the preserve, usually open from 9:00 A.M. to 5:00 P.M. daily all year. But it's a good idea to call beforehand and ask about the eagle-sighting situation. The preserve also has a great series of nature lectures and demonstrations by trained naturalists.

Don't let winter scare you off, because the preserve has 7 miles of intermediate ranked trails for cross-county skiing opportunities that get you fairly close to the viewing sites. On winter weekends, a chartered bus can take visitors to eagle habitats elsewhere in the county as well, but the prime locales in the preserve are not readily accessible to those with disabilities in the off-season. The trails near the migration sites are difficult to maneuver.

Continue east on Highway 60 to Boscobel and the yellow limestone **Boscobel Hotel,** where the Gideon Bible Society was founded in 1898. A group of local businessmen formed the Christian Commercial Men's Association of America, more commonly known as the Gideons, International. They thought it would be important to place Bibles in hotel rooms to keep traveling salesmen on the straight and narrow. Since that time, the society has distributed more than 10 million Bibles to lodgings around the country.

The hotel is a funky, comfortable old place that was recently remodeled with period antiques. The owners, however, decided to cash in and move back home to California and put the place up for sale. But you can still drive past the hotel with its high arched windows and plain facade at 1005 Wisconsin Avenue. And, yes, there are—or were—Gideon Bibles in each room.

Immediately off Wisconsin Avenue in Boscobel is the last remaining ❖ **Grand Army of the Republic (GAR) Hall** in the state. Built in the 1880s, the building has been left as it was when Civil War veterans met there to reminisce about their salad days in uniform. Plenty of memorabilia and regimental documents pack the display cases.

The hall is open at irregular hours, so it's a hit-or-miss proposition. Yet for any Civil War fan, an attempt is worth it. You'll probably be lucky.

From Boscobel, take off to Highland, driving southeast via County Roads S to T to M to Q. From Highland, go west 4 miles on Highway Q to Pine Tree Road, then north to the ◆**Spurgeon Vineyards and Winery** for a sample of their various vintages (608–929–7692). The vineyards are open from 10:00 A.M. to 5:00 P.M. daily, April 1 to December 1, and the same hours on weekends only the rest of the year.

Spurgeon grows such American grape varieties as the Concord and Delaware, in addition to French hybrids such as Rosette and Aurora. Prices of the distinctively labeled wines range from $5.50 to $.6.50, a dollar less per bottle if you purchase by the case. There's no charge for the tour and tasting.

From the vineyards, return to Highland and drive south on Highway 80 to the tiny community of Cobb. Go west from Cobb to Fennimore. Just before hitting Main Street, turn left on Highway 61 and go the two blocks or so to the ◆**Fennimore Cheese Factory** (608–822–6416). Stock up on samples of Bahl Baby Swiss and watch the morning cheese-making process between 9:00 A.M. and 5:00 P.M. Monday through Saturday and between 10:00 A.M. and 4:00 P.M. Sunday. There's an observation ramp where you can easily observe the activity. The factory also makes Colby, Cheddar, and Monterey Jack varieties.

The ◆**Fennimore Doll Museum** (608–922–4100) has more than 5,000 dolls representing a span of generations. The dolls are made of wood, cloth, plastic, ceramic, and even stone, collected over the years by a local farm woman who wanted them to be available for viewing in her hometown, rather than in some big-city museum. Anyone who thinks dolls are too feminine will get a kick out of the display of Star Wars figurines and John Wayne and Roy Rogers action characters. But the biggest attraction is probably the Barbie collection, which covers the thirty-plus years from the first leggy, buxom doll to the most contemporary. All her friends and accoutrements are shown off as well. The museum, on the city's main street, opposite the parking lot for the Silent Woman Restaurant, is open daily from spring through late autumn. Hours vary, so it is best to call ahead. Admission is charged.

The Fenmore Hills Motel, 2 miles west of town on Old Highway 18, boasts "unique bridal suites." If you want to try out the circular waterbed, give the place a call at (608) 822–3281. That room costs weekend guests $105, but the rate is a mere $85 Sundays through Thursdays. A regular room, with steam bath, runs $48. Add a bathroom with a whirlpool for $51. Take your cheese along, and don't forget the Spurgeon wine.

After munching your fill at the cheese factory and/or lolling on the waterbed, continue south out of Fennimore on Highway 61 to Lancaster for a peek at the ❖ **Grant County Courthouse.** The imposing structure, in the middle of the town square, has a copper and glass double dome modeled after St. Peter's Basilica in Rome.

The square is also the site of the first Civil War monument erected in the United States, according to local lore. The statue was dedicated on July 4, 1867, after a private and county fund drive.

The "great, big, tall" monument (as proudly described by Lancaster citizens) is on the northeast side of the square and consists of a central marble pillar surrounded by eight smaller pillars. The memorial is inscribed with the names of 755 Grant County soldiers who either died or were injured during the Civil War. Don't confuse that monument with the one erected in 1906 by the ladies' auxiliary of the Grand Army of the Republic. They put up a statue of a soldier atop a pedestal on the northwest side of the courthouse.

On the southeast corner is a statue of Grant County resident Nelson Dewey, who was the county's first clerk of courts in 1836 and Wisconsin's first governor in 1848. Dewey is perched importantly in a chair, looking appropriately governorlike. Dewey's Lancaster home is located at 147 W. Hickory Street, now occupied by an insurance agency. I've been told the folks there will probably let you peek around a bit, if you come during business hours.

Look at the display on the first floor of the courthouse featuring the county's collection of Civil War memorabilia. Much of it was donated by the family of General John Clark, the town's resident Civil War general—long deceased, of course. Among the artifacts is a captured Confederate battle flag.

After spending an hour or two wandering around Lancaster (having lunch either in the **Arrow Restaurant** or the historic **Lancaster House Hotel**), follow Highway 61 south to 133, which leads to Potosi, an old lead mining boom town tucked into a deep, skinny valley.

Around the War of 1812, most of the lead mined in the country came from this region. Several of the villages were larger than Chicago and Milwaukee at the time. Today, all you see are the remains of pits and furnaces where the mostly Welsh and Cornish miners set up camp. The state's nickname, "The Badger State," came from these early miners. Let me explain. When the men first moved to the vicinity, prior to building barracks, they dug shallow trenches in the hillsides to get away from the rain. The holes served as protection from marauding Indians as well, since they were always dug near another miner's hideaway for a musket crossfire. In calmer days, visitors saw these holes in the slopes and likened them to badger burrows, hence the state's nickname. Some of these pits, framed by low stone barricades, can be seen on the hillsides around Potosi.

The workmen who went south in the winter, when some of the mines closed for the season, were called "suckers," after a type of Mississippi River fish.

There are about forty crumbled old buildings, open pit mines, smelters, and huts scattered around the vicinity of the one-street town, once the leading port on the northern Mississippi. By 1833, more than 237 steamboats were making regular stops at Potosi landing. River towns along this stretch of the Mississippi all the way to Fort Snelling in St. Paul, Minnesota, used the town as a storage facility for whiskey, flour, trade goods, bacon, and munitions. The boats would leave the docks laden with lead, heading for New Orleans and ocean-bound freighters. Hardswearing teamsters picked up the supplies the paddle wheelers dropped off and hauled them inland, using huge carts pulled by ten oxen at a time over muddy trails.

"Ripley's Believe It or Not" column of years ago said that Potosi's main street was the longest in the world without an intersection. It extended some 5 miles through the valley, linking the scattered mining sites and ethnic enclaves such as British Hollow (built by the English) and Van Buren (home for Dutch settlers). There's not much there now, except for scattered gas stations and several antique stores. Developers have considered refurbishing the battered but still serviceable Potosi Brewery building into a complex of craft shops or even reopening it as a brewery.

The **St. John Mine** (608–763–2121) in Potosi is open for summer touring, after a succession of owners attempted to make it into a tourist attraction. Stories about the mine date from 1640 when French explorers found Winnebagos living there and mining lead for trade. After a peace treaty was signed with local Winnebago tribes in 1827, miners poured into southwestern Wisconsin. One intrepid soul who became rich during those rough-and-tumble lead mining days was Willis St. John, after whom the largest mine was named. Mining in the vicinity died out during the Gold Rush of 1849, but there was a resurgence throughout the Civil War. In that conflict, Wisconsin's mines provided most of the lead for the Northern armies. The lead deposits eventually petered out, and the St. John mine officially closed in 1870.

Today, watch your step in walking up the steep slope to the cavern and be sure to take comfortable walking shoes if you plan to enter the mine. Once inside, you can still see the pick and chisel marks on the walls made in those early days. It's an eerie feeling.

There's good canoeing along the Grant, Big Platte, and Little Platte rivers near Potosi. It's best to bring your own equipment because of the difficulty in finding an outfitter who keeps in business from year to year. Among the better put-in spots along the Grant is one at Klondike Springs on the left bank of County Trunk K. That can give you a nineteen-hour run downstream to the Potosi boat landing on the Mississippi if your muscles are so inclined.

Louthain Bridge on the right bank of County Trunk B is a fine set-off on the Big Platte. For the Little Platte, try the Church Road Bridge (right bank on Church Road), Shinoe Bridge (where Highways 61 and 35 intersect—use the right bank), or the Banfield Bridge public boat landing.

Rollo Jameson, a Beetown farmer/repair shop owner/tavernkeeper/janitor, had a fever for collecting just about anything. He filled sheds with "valuables," organizing his finds into categories: stoves, vending machines, farm machinery, and so on. When the ninety-three-year-old Jameson died in 1981, the city of Platteville took over the assemblage of oddities and moved everything to the old high school where it can currently be viewed.

Now called the Rollo Jameson Museum, the school building at 405 E. Main Street is open from 9:00 A.M. to 5:00 P.M. daily, May 1 through October 31. It is also open from 9:00 A.M. to 4:00 P.M. Monday through Friday from November through April.

Next door to the Jameson place is the ◆ **Platteville Mining Museum,** where visitors can descend ninety, count 'em, ninety steps down into a shaft of the **Bevans Lead Mine,** reopened in 1976. Above ground, rides are given on a train of ore cars pulled by a restored mine locomotive. For those with phobias about knocking their heads on the ceiling, hard hats are standard issue at the entrance. The museum is open from 9:00 A.M. to 5:00 P.M. Monday through Friday, May 1 until the end of October, and from 9:00 A.M. to 4:00 P.M. daily, November 1 to April 30. Tours of the mine are offered only May through October, with the exception of reserved groups. There is a small admission charge. The museum, located in a refurbished schoolhouse, is at 405 E. Main Street (608–348–3301).

The mine was discovered in 1845 by Lorenzo Bevans, who had used his life's resources and was in debt up to his high-brow nose while searching for lead. On a mid-July day of that year, he could afford to pay his hired hand only until noon. But the fellow agreed to stay on until the end of the day. At 2:00 that afternoon, the two men broke into one of the richest veins of lead ever discovered in southwestern Wisconsin.

Before leaving Grant County, check out the **Dickeyville Grotto,** built by parish priest Father Mathias Wernerus. The dedicated clergyman assembled bottles, stone, glass, and other cast-off artifacts to make his shrine, spending from 1925 to 1929 collecting, hauling, and cementing the whole thing together. "We built better than we knew" was his motto. About seven carloads of rock were taken from quarries around the Midwest, with other stones coming from every state and from the Holy Land. Some Chippewa Indians from northern Wisconsin even donated arrowheads and axes for inclusion in one section. The grotto, on the east and south sides of Holy Cross Church, is located at 305 Main Street (608–568–7519). Hours are 9:00 A.M. to 6:00 P.M. daily April 15 through October. Donations are accepted. Father Wernerus's grave is in the rear of the church.

In addition to Father Wernerus's glittering, ponderous masterpiece, Dickeyville is noted for its more secular May and September motorcycle and four-wheel-drive hill climbs and tractor pulls.

Not that all roads lead to Dickeyville, but most do in this corner of Wisconsin. To get to this old German farming community, take either Highways 61, 35, or 151.

## GREEN COUNTY

Folks in Green County brag that their landscape is a Little Switzerland. They certainly are correct when it comes to driving over hills and dales that could easily pass for alpine meadows. For this reason, thousands of Swiss émigrés settled here in the 1800s. Their tidy homesteads polkadot the countryside, where cows outnumber people five to three.

In 1986, Green County celebrated its 150th anniversary, a fete topped off by the opening of the refurbished courthouse in Monroe, the county seat. The town's fund-raisers, "The Steeple People," collected nearly $50,000 for the restoration of the building's ornate tower and its four-sided clock.

But Monroe isn't just a place to sit on your hands in the town square and watch the time pass. The community hosts the annual county fair, something that it's been doing since 1853. In late July, the exposition of giant vegetables, nose-wriggling rabbits, beefy cattle, rounds of delicious cheese, grandma's pickles, and 4-H crafts creates a lot of hoopla for celebrating farm life.

For an added summertime twist, the citizenry organized a Hot Air Balloon Rally several years ago. The event was so popular, it now draws aeronauts from around the country. Balloonists are attracted by the grand notion of sweeping over the county's bright green valleys and hills. Get all the details on dates by contacting the Monroe Chamber of Commerce, 648 Eighth Street (608–325–7648).

A not-miss visit in Monroe is a stop at the ❖**Jos. Huber Brewing Company,** in business since Wisconsin became a state in 1848. Free tours are offered daily here, at one of the few small, privately owned breweries remaining in the state. Samples of the clear, light Huber brews are *de rigueur,* of course.

Say "lactobacillus bulgaricus" in Monroe, and nobody's eyebrows will go up. The bacteria is one of the starters in manufacturing Swiss cheese, an economic mainstay in the Monroe area with its twenty-three factories (a total of thirty-six are in the county).

The limestone subsoil makes this heart of Wisconsin's dairyland rich in the right kind of milk for Muenster, Limburger, and other cheese varieties, as well as Swiss. The county's Holsteins and Brown Swiss are truly contented cows.

Many of the plants in the county allow visitors, but you have to be on hand by noon, or most of the day's work will be over.

**15**

The factories kick into yawning gear around 5:00 A.M. For a list of licensed outlets, write Cheese Days, Box 606, Monroe 53566. The plants, all members of the Foreign Type Cheesemakers Association (FTCA), are headquartered in town. The members sponsor the Monroe Cheese Days, held in September every even-numbered year. These Big Cheeses of the county's agricultural community offer an average of eleven tons of the stuff for nibbling at these events. When they say, "Cheese," they mean it! The festival features a Cheesemaker's Kickoff Ball, Cheese Day Chase marathon run, cheese-making demonstrations, factory tours, and, of course, lots of cheese sandwiches.

One of the top bike jaunts in Wisconsin is along the new 23.5-mile-long ◆ **Sugar River Trail,** which meanders through the county along an abandoned railroad right-of-way. The route opened in 1986 and has yet to "be discovered" by hordes of outsiders.

Cyclists eighteen and over need a trail permit, however, which can be obtained at Sugar River headquarters at the New Glarus Woods State Park, Box 781, New Glarus 53574 (608–527–2334). Bikes can be rented at the park, but car shuttle service is not available.

The gently rolling grade is barely 1 percent, making it a great trip for short-legged kids. For puffing oldsters, there are plenty of pit stops along the way in New Glarus, Monticello, Albany, and Brodhead. Better than Epsom salts is a foot soak in the Sugar River where a covered bridge spans the stream near Brodhead. It's also a good place to hunker down while waiting out a rainstorm. The ford is one of fourteen along the route as the trail zigzags back and forth across the river and its tributaries. The route is also excellent for fervid cross-country skiers during Wisconsin's blustery winters. Midway between connecting points of New Glarus on the north and Brodhead on the south is the **Albany Wildlife Refuge.** Look for the herons and other bird life that inhabit the reeds and woodlands. The Sugar River Trail is also part of the 1,000-mile-long **Ice Age National Scenic Trail** that connects routes throughout Wisconsin.

New Glarus probably epitomizes all those Green County placemat images of Switzerland. Settled by pioneers from the Swiss canton of Glarus in 1845, the town remains small. Only about 1,700 citizens live here, so it's not hard to find your way around. In the summer, downtown shops and many homes feature window boxes exploding with crimson geraniums.

Many of the houses in the community date from the turn of the century, and a ◆ **Swiss historical village** on the west side of town shows how life was on the Wisconsin frontier prior to the Civil War. The cluster of buildings at 612 Seventh Avenue (608–527–2921) is open from 9:00 A.M. to 5:00 P.M. daily, May through October. The last tour is conducted at 4:30 P.M. Admission is $4.00 for adults and $1.00 for children five to twelve.

The townspeople harken back to their heritage with locally staged summertime productions of *Heidi,* the famed folktale of the Swiss mountain girl, and *Wilhelm Tell,* of apple-shooting fame. Women from New Glarus have made all the costumes for the shows, staged in the town's outdoor amphitheater. Don't despair in case of rain. With inclement weather, the shows are readily moved to the high school auditorium.

Outgoing Swiss-born hosteler Hans Lenzlinger owns and manages the New Glarus Hotel (608–527–5244), a chalet-style hostelry bedecked with flowers hanging everywhere from heavy wooden balconies.

For a varied New Glarus/Green County munch other than cheese, try Flannery's **Wilhelm Tell Supper Club,** featuring a respectably extensive Swiss menu. The club is located at 114 Second Street. You will need to call for weekend reservations (608–527–2618).

You can load up on typical souvenirs at the town's several gift shops, but for a special keepsake, the **Swiss Miss Lace Factory and Textile Mart** has some out-of-this-world embroideries and lace.

## IOWA COUNTY

Nope, you aren't in the wrong state when you come to Iowa. The county is in the heart of the Hidden Valleys tourism area of southwestern Wisconsin. Mineral Point, a prime jumping-off spot for an off-the-beaten-path adventure, is one of the oldest communities in the state. It was founded in 1827 by lead miners who easily scooped up the precious metal from surface pits near the town. Evidence of their digging can be spotted from any backcountry roads in the vicinity.

Peek into the miners' past at Mineral Point's ◆ **Pendarvis,** a complex of restored cabins built by settlers from Cornwall more than 150 years ago when the streets of southwestern Wisconsin were paved with zinc and lead, not gold. The new

**17**

arrivals immediately began quarrying Galena limestone for use in their cottages.

Walking along Tamblyn's Row, a stretch of rowhouses, you'd think you were back in England. Shake Rag Alley is typical of the street names. Its moniker is derived from the practice of the miners' wives' waving their aprons or dish towels from the house windows when lunch was ready. The Pendarvis property was acquired by the state historical society in 1971. It is open from 9:00 A.M. to 5:00 P.M. daily, May through October. Guided tours are offered as well (608–987–2122). The last tour leaves at 4:00 P.M. The facility is administered by the State Historical Society of Wisconsin.

Admission is $5.00 for adults and $2.00 for youngsters ages five to twelve. Discount rates of $4.50 are offered for seniors and AAA members. Bring ten or more friends with a reservation and utilize the $4.00-per-head group rate.

While in the neighborhood, try a Cornish pasty (*past-ee*), a meat pie with a thin crust that the worker would take with him to the mine facing. Most of the town's bakeries and restaurants offer the ethnic delicacies. Try one at the **Chesterfield Inn,** 20 Commerce Street, in Mineral Point (608–987–3682). The inn is a refurbished stagecoach stop dating from 1834. Pasties and other Cornish fare are on the menu. The restaurant has an outdoor patio for casual dining on summer evenings. Prices are moderate.

Take Highway 151 from Mineral Point to Dodgeville, seat of Iowa County and home of the state's oldest courthouse, which dates from 1859. South of Dodgeville about 2 miles just off Highway 18 is the ◆**Folklore Village** (608–924–3725), which offers regular Saturday night folk dancing and singing programs in the old Wakefield Schoolhouse. The place is the brainchild of Jane Farwell, who usually is on hand wearing Tyrolean peasant clothing. Since the 1940s, Jane has set up folk dance camps and seminars around the country, bringing that expertise with her to Wisconsin in the mid-1960s. Throughout the week, craft demonstrations, programs for youngsters, and music lessons are held. Holiday time is ongoing. Scandinavian midsummer feasts, Ukrainian and Greek Easters, Israeli Purim, husking bees, and others fill the calendar.

Drive north of Dodgeville on Highway 23 to the ◆**FantaSuite Don Q Resort.** You'll know that you've arrived after spotting the grounded Boeing prop C-97 parked alongside the highway.

The ninety-ton beast was flown to the site, parked there, and left as is by the resort's flamboyant former owner, Ron Dentinger. A 67-foot-high tree made of steel wagon wheels has also been erected outside the building, just in case somebody misses the plane while driving past.

The Don Q is one of the kinds of places that make a weekend away a something-else eyebrow-raising treat. One of the rooms is in a spire from an old Methodist Church adjacent to the main complex. On the bottom floor of the steeple are the bathroom facilities; on the second level is a queen-sized bed; on the third is a stereo complex, a pile of pillows, and windows for the best view (if you're looking) at the countryside around Dodgeville. It's a great place to try an in-spire-ed "let down your long hair" routine on your lady love. Sixteen of the Don Q's forty-six suites have hanging beds, baths made from copper cheese vats, and assorted similar delightfully kinky wonders. Try the Float Room, with a queen-sized waterbed set in a Viking ship, a heart-shaped hydrotherapy tub, and mirrors on the wall ($94; $79 Sunday through Thursday). Or how about Tranquillity Base, featuring a re-creation of a Gemini space capsule and a ten-sided waterbed ($165; $225 Friday and Saturday). The restaurant on the premises is a salvaged barn.

Just before you get to the Don Q is the **Walnut Hollow Farm,** which turned a cottage corporation into a national business, growing from 5 employees to 129 in fifteen years. Walnut Hollow is on Highway 23 North.

Using cross sections of tree limbs harvested in the state, Walnut Hollow makes several hundred products for the wood craft industry. A showroom offers clock-making and wood-burning supplies, which can be up to 70 percent off retail prices. The dozens of examples of finely honed woodburned etchings on display always make me wonder why my dabbling never turns out so well. Walnut Hollow is open from 9:00 A.M. to 6:00 P.M. Mondays through Saturdays and from 11:00 A.M. to 4:00 P.M. Sundays.

Immediately to the north of the Don Q is the entrance to **Governor Dodge State Park,** a sprawling preserve of 5,000 acres, with two lakes, camping sites, hiking trails, and fishing spots.

Nearby is Spring Green's **House on the Rock,** a home perched on a pinnacle of stone called Deershelter Rock, 450 feet above the floor of Wyoming Valley near the Baraboo Range. The home was built in the 1940s by Alex Jordan, a noted Wisconsin sculptor and art collector. It was opened to the public in 1961.

A musical museum and the world's largest carousel (weighing in at thirty-five tons and standing 80 feet high) are located at the base of the rock. Most of the home is open for touring, with passageways cut through the rock and neat nooks and crannies set aside for reading, loafing, or peering out over the countryside far below.

Jordan had a penchant for doing big things. The central fire pit is large enough to roast a woolly mammoth (critters that actually roamed the valley a few millennia before the House on the Rock was built).

The buildings are open for touring from April 1 to October 31. Tickets go on sale at 8:00 A.M., with the last tickets being sold about two hours prior to early evening closing, due to the time it takes to tour the complex. Hours vary from spring to summer; call (608) 935–3639 for more information. Admission is $3.50 for kids ages four to six, $8.50 for youngsters seven to twelve, and $13.50 for ages thirteen and over. A group of twenty or more persons can get a tour rate of $11.50 per person. Sales tax will be added to the admission price.

The Spring Green area (Iowa and Sauk counties along the Wisconsin River) was called home by famed architect Frank Lloyd Wright, who worked there on his uncle's farm as a kid. The crusty, eccentric, and brilliant Wright built his home, **Taliesin,** into the brow of a hill near the Wisconsin River (Iowa County). The building is not open to the public, but other Wright structures in the area are.

Before you get to the junction of Highway 23 and County Road C is the Wright-designed ✦**Hillside Home School** (Iowa County), which includes a drafting studio and galleries displaying some of the builder's notable designs. The school is open for visitors from late June through Labor Day. Tours run every half hour from 10:00 A.M. to 4:00 P.M. Admission is charged. For information call (608) 588–2511.

Folks in Spring Green still reminisce about the master architect's strolling about the town as if he owned it. Although Wright died in 1959, the town of Spring Green in Sauk County remains the headquarters for Taliesin Associated Architects and the Frank Lloyd Wright School of Architecture. Buildings designed by the architectural firm include the Valley Bank in downtown Spring

Green. To see other Wright buildings, stop at the **Spring Green Restaurant** on Highway 23 along the banks of the Wisconsin River (608–588–2571) or swing past **Wyoming Valley School,** 4 miles south of Taliesin on Highway 23. The last two are in Iowa County.

While in the Spring Green area, turn east on C off Highway 14 to get to the ◆**American Players Theater.** Its resident troupe presents Shakespearean productions and other classics during the summer.

Bring bug repellent and dress for the weather because seating is under the open sky. There's something fantastic about watching *Midsummer Night's Dream* with an umbrella of stars. The theater was constructed by Korean-American actor Randall Duk Kim and his associates in 1980. For a time, the company was treading thin financial ice, but a concerted marketing effort and aggressive ticket promotions saved the day. With the crowds, you'll now need to have reservations. Contact the theater at Box 819, Spring Green 53588 (608–588–7401) for the year's production lineup.

For the best in relaxation, try the ◆**Springs Golf Club Resort** (800–822–7774), across the country road from the American Players Theater. It is one of the classiest resorts in western Wisconsin, with a gourmet chef, family health club programs, and—of course—golf, golf, golf. There is a Wright feel to the place, with its rooms and interior furnishings that bespeak comfort without overstating it. And there is space for skis, golf clubs, and other outdoor gear as well, along with a microwave, refrigerator, and kitchen nook in each suite. The Springs hosts a gourmet nature trek each autumn (call for the date), where the wines of Rhinehessia or New South Wales might be served with a pheasant pâté and Wisconsin cheese at one trail stop, a cold cucumber soup and black bread at another, chocolate-covered strawberries and mile-high cheesecake at the next. And so it goes for the entire length of the trudge across the maple-shrouded ridges behind the resort. Eat as much as you want; you will wear off any calories picked up along the way.

## LA CROSSE COUNTY

La Crosse County marks the northwestern boundary of the Hidden Valleys tourism region. The city of La Crosse, population 50,000, is the largest in the western part of Wisconsin. The

French named the site after watching a rough-and-tumble Indian game that utilized long-handled racquets.

The competition reminded the trappers of the aristocratic game of tennis, called *la crosse*. A statue by Elmer Peterson in front of the La Crosse Radisson Hotel depicts several Indians swinging into action during a spirited match.

A good place to keep an eye on all the folks in town is from atop the 500-foot **Grandad's Bluff** on the east side of the city. From the sharp drop-off, the flatlands leading to the Mississippi look like a slightly rumpled bedsheet covered with toy houses and crisscrossed by tiny cars.

To get to the bluff, take Main Street through town toward Hixon Forest. It's quite a drive up to the parking lots near the crest, but some tough bikers always seem to be puffing their way upwards.

Not me. I've always preferred to drive and arrive refreshed. Telescopes at the far end of the observation platform can be used to spot La Crosse landmarks, such as the city's meeting center, the G. Heileman Brewery grain elevators, and the playing fields of the University of Wisconsin–La Crosse. As for the last, you'll get better seats in the stadium stands for viewing athletic events. But it's a challenge to try to pick out which football team is which from that distance. Look for the varied colored jerseys. About midway up the roadway in the rear of Grandad's Bluff is a refreshment stand for quick sandwiches and soda.

From Interstate 90 take Highway 53 south to State Street west to Riverside Park, where the La Crosse and Black rivers join the Mississippi. At the north end of the park is ◆ **Riverside USA** with an animated display focusing on the history of the Mississippi River. At the park, kids can try their hands at captaining a riverboat, the *Belle of La Crosse*. The pilothouse is a reproduction of what an actual vessel would look and sound like. Riverside USA is open from 10:00 A.M. to 5:00 P.M. daily during the summer.

From the park, take a ninety-minute cruise on the real thing, the *La Crosse Queen*. The 300-passenger stern-wheeler departs regularly for cruises along the river. Perching on the upper deck, leaning back in a chair, and admiring the sun's rays dancing across the water is a grand way to laze away a summer afternoon.

Some years back, a friend and I eyed a more rugged approach to the river. We took a small duckboat, loaded it with camping gear at a La Crosse dock, and aimed downstream for a week's

*La Crosse Queen*

adventure. Cruising past the 25-foot-tall, twenty-five-ton Big Indian statue at the confluence of the La Crosse, Black, and Mississippi rivers, we waved goodbye to comfort for a week. Of course, it was late autumn. The wind was fierce, the rain crept up under our ponchos, and the fish weren't biting. But that was all still ahead of us as we set off. Now, older and just a bit wiser, I'd still take such a jaunt out of town, but I'd probably do it in the summer aboard a houseboat.

Here are two that offer good deals: Captain's Cruises, 710 Division Street, La Crosse 54601 (608–784–3088), and Great River Cruises, 400 Winona Street, La Crosse 54601 (608–783–3879 or 783–1697).

The city's nationally known fall festival, Oktoberfest, is held during the last weekend in September. Capitalizing on the Germanic heritage of many of its current residents, the venue includes plenty of polka parties, beer tents, and grilled bratwurst.

You can't miss seeing the world's largest six-pack of beer, outside the **G. Heileman Brewing Company,** 925 South Third Street (608–785–1000). The tanks hold enough beer to fill 7,340,796 cans of Old Style. Placed end to end, the row of cans would cover 565 miles, according to the brewery. Regular tours of the plant are offered year-round.

Winter is a good time to come to the La Crosse area. There are numerous cross-country ski trails that range from beginner to advanced. Try pathways near the city in Hixon Forest, Blue Bird Springs, Goose Island, and Perrot State Park. For trail guides, contact the La Crosse Convention and Visitors Bureau, 410 E. Veterans Memorial Drive, La Crosse 54602 (608–782–2366).

Downhill skiing is pretty good at **Mount La Crosse,** 2 miles south of the city on Highway 35. The hill has a 516-foot vertical drop and a run of 5,300 feet.

West of La Crosse on Highway 16, about a mile or so north of Interstate 94, is **West Salem,** home of pioneer author Hamlin Garland. The bushy-haired, Pulitzer Prize–winning novelist was born here in 1860 and returned when he was an adult. He wrote dozens of short stories and novels about the farmers and other people who lived in the "coulee country" of La Crosse County. A coulee is a valley, usually with very steep sides. Among his best known works were *Son of the Middle Border* and *Main-Traveled Roads.*

When Garland moved to Iowa late in his life, my poet father became friends with the old storyteller, who offered many good-humored suggestions on writing styles. Garland's West Salem house is located at 357 W. Garland Street (608–786–1399) and is open 10:00 A.M. to 4:30 P.M. Memorial Day to Labor Day. Admission is charged.

The West Salem Rustic Road, accessible from Interstate 90 at the town's freeway exit, is the only one in the state featuring a residential area within a major stretch of its 2.5-mile route. The road edges past the home of Thomas Leonard, founder of West Salem; the village's main business district; Garland's homestead; the Octagon House (on the National Register of Historic Places) at the corner of Highways C and 16; and Swarthout Lakeside Park.

## LAFAYETTE COUNTY

The little community of Belmont, where today's Highway 126 bisects 151, can brag about its flirt with history in 1836. At the time, settlers were casting about for a capital of the Wisconsin Territory. Since the population was equally spread through what is now Iowa, the Dakotas, Wisconsin, and Minnesota, there was a lot of argument about the best locale. Governor Henry Dodge picked Belmont because of its centralized location and because it wasn't far from his own home. The choice received so much criticism that Dodge retreated and allowed the territorial representatives to suggest alternative locations. Subsequently, the capital was moved to Iowa for a time before coming back to Wisconsin. Madison eventually won the nod and continued as capital when Wisconsin was made a state.

But the ◆ **First Capitol State Park and Museum** recalls that nineteenth-century controversy. Drive 3 miles north of Belmont on Highway G to the park, operated by the Lafayette County Historical Society. The emotional air is calmer now, and the long-forgotten debate is far removed from the minds of picnickers and hikers on the trails.

Speaking of capitals, the **Lafayette County Courthouse** in Darlington was built in 1905 through the generosity of local mining magnate Matthew Murphy. Financed through his will, the imposing limestone structure features a central rotunda and an elaborately painted dome. Marble walls and fancy woodwork round off the building.

Guests are free to wander the halls and study the graceful architectural style at their leisure. The county clerk requests, however, that visitors come during the week's regular working hours.

Lafayette County is geared for outdoors enthusiasts. ◆ **Blackhawk Memorial County Park** in Woodford annually hosts a black powder shoot and Indian encampment in May, sponsored by the Yellowstone Flint and Cap Blackpowder Club. Adding variety to the program are tomahawk throwing and a candle shoot. Although we're black powder shooters ourselves, using a smoothbore Brown Bess musket patterned after the regulation British army piece of the Revolutionary War, I've never participated in the Blackhawk rendezvous. But the event is highly recommended by buckskinning friends who have enjoyed the reenactment.

Just to the north, along Highway 78, is **Yellowstone Lake State Park** near Blanchardville (608–523–4427). The 445-acre lake is the focus of the park's activities. In the winter, a 12-mile public snowmobile trail connects the park to Darlington. Each June, the city hosts a 10-mile canoe race along the Pecatonica River with twenty categories for its hundreds of contestants. With odds like that, even landlubbing duffers like me who spend more time bumping into riverbanks than cruising merrily along have a chance to snare a trophy.

To help in this regard, Lafayette County's historic churches stand ready. In 1844 missionary Father Samuel Mazzuchelli built a neat wooden church in **New Diggings,** a lead mining town in the western section of the county. Serving the "badgers" in the neighborhood, hearty Mazzuchelli tromped through the woods to encourage his rough-and-tumble frontier flock to attend mass.

In the other end of the county, Lutheran pastors founded the East Wiota Lutheran Church in 1844. The church is still being used by descendants of Norwegian settlers who lived here in those days. The tidy, trim building is the oldest Norwegian Lutheran Church in North America and is still used as parish.

Like its neighboring counties, Lafayette County was born and weaned during those heady lead rush days that extended from the late 1820s to the 1840s. Hub of the county's mining and commercial world was Shullsburg.

The county lies at the southern edge of the glacial movement that pancaked most of Wisconsin eons ago. Geologists call the vicinity west of town a "driftless area" because it was never smoothed under the towering plates of ice. The deep, dark valleys and moody ridgetops that were untouched by the ice are obvious while driving along Highway 11. Since the glaciers never dispersed or buried the lead deposits, early miners found fairly easy pickings.

The ◆ **Badger Mine Museum,** 279 Estey Street (608–965–4860), takes visitors into that era with an extensive display of old-time mining gear. The museum, on the site of the Badger Lot Diggings that began operations in 1827, is open from 9:00 A.M. to 5:00 P.M. daily from Memorial Day through Labor Day. Admission is charged.

The men who worked in the Diggings labored twelve hours a day for the princely sum of $1. They were lowered by windlass 40 to 50 feet underground, where they crawled on hands and knees to the lead facings in the rock. Working by candlelight, these stocky Cornishmen could seldom stand completely upright, even though most of the men were barely over 5 feet tall. Visitors have it easier now, although they are still 47 feet under the surface. You can stand up straight in parts of the mine traversed during the quarter-mile tour.

The miners believed that a form of goblin, the Cornish Knockers, had followed them from tin mines in the Old Country and lived in the darkest recesses of the New World caverns.

Generally, the Knockers would make their appropriate tap-tap sound to indicate a rich mineral vein. In exchange, the miners had to leave a bit of their luncheon pasty as a thank you. If they didn't receive such a gift, the angry Knockers could cause mine roofs to collapse. Don't worry about that today—there haven't been any reports of Cornish Knockers in the Shullsburg vicinity since the Badger Lot Diggings closed in 1856.

Shullsburg itself is a community designed for strolling. Park anywhere and amble along winding streets with such lilting names as Hope, Charity, Friendship, and Justice. Originally, the roads were mere paths followed by miners from their homes to the shafts and were named by the good Dominican friar, Father Mazzuchelli, on one of his Bible-thumping jaunts through town.

## MONROE COUNTY

The earliest of the state's major bike paths, the famed ◆ **Elroy-Sparta Trail,** opened in 1966 and annually hosts more than 55,000 riders. Since the trail is on an old railroad bed, you'll even travel through three century-old tunnels that save you the legwork you would have needed for steeper grades. The trail wanders for 32.5 miles across Monroe County into Juneau County. During the summer, all-you-can-eat pancake breakfasts are served in the Wilton Municipal Park. The breakfasts, put on by the Lions Club, run from Memorial Day weekend until Labor Day. Wilton is about the mid-way point on the ride. For information on bike rentals, auto shuttles, campgrounds, and other lodging and restaurant listings, contact the Elroy-Sparta State Trail, Box 153, Kendall 54638 (608–463–7109). Highway 71 parallels the trail for almost the entire route, which makes it convenient for tired riders who need to be picked up.

Don't be surprised if you are driving through Angelo, just a hop and a jump north of Sparta, and a giant eagle appears to be taking wing from a parking lot. Look twice and you might see an elephant, a monster gorilla, a huge beaver, or some other bigger-than-life creature. There's no cause to worry, however, since the pack of critters is nothing more than completed products, produced by F.A.S.T. Corp., headquartered in Sparta.

The acronym stands for ◆ **Fiberglass Animals, Shapes and Trademarks,** which makes the animals for displays around the world. They're often kept outside the plant until ready for shipping. As a result, F.A.S.T. President Jerry Vettrus is used to cars screeching to a halt in front of his place.

If you're so inclined, you can purchase something big for the backyard pool. How about a spouting whale or a leaping muskie? It'll probably cost about $2,000 for something under 20 feet tall. But wouldn't it be worth it?

## RICHLAND COUNTY

Richland Center hosts the ◆ **Wisconsin High School Rodeo Association Championships** each June at the Richland County fairgrounds on County Road AA on the city's north side. Kids from around the state compete in calf roping, bulldogging, bronc riding, barrel racing, and other bone-jarring events. Some of the youngsters eventually go on to college rodeo teams and then to the pro circuit. Call or stop by the chamber of commerce downtown office (608–647–6205), located in a 1937 Pullman railroad car. They'll also be able to tell you about the tractor pulls held at the county fairgrounds each July. Some of the heavy equipment operators can haul 12,000 pounds or more over a set course on the dirt track.

Take Highway 40 north about 7 miles to Rockbridge to **Pier Natural Bridge Park,** site of one of the first white settlements in Richland County. There are scenic rock formations all along Highways 80, 60, 58, and 56, which spin around Rockbridge like spokes. The park's main feature is a long bridge of rock, at least 60 feet high and 80 feet wide.

If spelunking is your thing, the county's **Eagle Cave** is another of the state's larger underground caverns. The cave is just off Highway 60, west of Eagle Corners. But if claustrophobia hits and subsurface roaming is not to your liking, there are 26.5 miles of hiking trails above the cave site. Eagle Cave is open to the public from Memorial Day to Labor Day, but the cave and grounds are used in the off-season by Scout troops. For more details, contact Eagle Cave, Route 2, Blue River 53518 (608–537–2988). To keep the crowds coming, the Wisconsin Skyrocket Coon Dog Field Trials are held here each June.

## VERNON COUNTY

About 38 miles north of Prairie du Chien on Highway 35, the

Great River Road, the Bad Axe River empties into the Mississippi. Here Black Hawk attempted to surrender his Sac and Fox followers to the white militia and Sioux warriors who had encamped at Fort Crawford. The troops, including Abraham Lincoln, ignored Black Hawk's white flag and chased the Indians into the river, where many drowned. The few survivors who made it across to the Iowa side were captured by the whites' Winnebago allies on the far bank and sent back to the fort, where they were imprisoned.

The site is the saddest along this stretch of the Mississippi, especially when autumn mists rise slowly out of the hollows along the roadway. You can feel the heaviness in the air before the harsh sun drives the fog away.

This is Vernon County, which was originally called Bad Axe County, but in 1861, image-conscious residents asked the state legislature to change the name to the less negative "Vernon," a loose Anglicizing of *verdant,* meaning "green." The legislators obliged, recalling the incident with Black Hawk, no doubt.

On a warm May day in 1990, the state of Wisconsin officially apologized for the massacre. Sac and Fox tribal leaders and state officials attended a ceremony held at a marker near the river indicating where much of the fighting took place. The sign is not far from what is now the village of Victory, named by white settlers to celebrate the military action. "The people who followed Black Hawk and didn't make it—maybe this will help put them to rest," said Sac and Fox Chief Elmer Manatowa.

The eastern portion of Vernon County has a large population of Amish, some of whom work in a furniture factory on County Road D northeast of Westby. Their creations of bent hickory rockers and other pieces are excellent. With the slow-moving Amish wagons on the county's backroads, motorists must be very careful. The highways through the area are notorious for curves and loops. Of course, the scenery compensates for the required slower-paced driving.

Trillium, a bed and breakfast in the heart of the Amish community, is a self-contained cottage where visitors can really get away from it all. For fresh-baked, homemade bread, owner Rosanne Boyett's touch is superb. Call (608) 625–4492.

The ◆ **Westby House** is another interesting bed and breakfast, located at 200 W. State Street in Westby (608–634–4112). The house is at the corner of Ramsland and State, only a block off

Highway 14. The Victorian-style 1890s home has six rooms, done up with antiques and crafts made throughout the area. Rates range from $55 to $80. All of the rooms (two with private bath) have queen-sized beds, and one, the Greenbriar, has two double beds. Kids are welcome. If you can't stay for the night, the public dining room offers a wide-ranging menu and is open for lunch and dinner throughout the week. Reservations are always recommended.

**Wildcat Mountain State Park** (608–337–4775) seems to appear out of nowhere, a mere twenty-minute ride west of Hillsboro on Highway 33. All of a sudden, there it is: deep gorges, pines, limestone cliffs, racing waterways to show a dramatically rugged side of Wisconsin.

Hillsboro itself is a quaint village that boasts its own museum, an 1860s log cabin on the northeast side of town. The little house is open from 1:00 to 4:00 P.M. Sundays from early June to Labor Day. By calling the city clerk at (608) 489–2521 or (608) 489–2192, you can probably get inside on other days. Half the building looks like an old post office, and the other half contains typical pioneer furnishings.

The **Inn at Wildcat Mountain** (608–337–4352) looks as if Mount Vernon was transplanted to the hill country. This is a large white house with massive pillars in front, located on the east side of the bridge leading over the Kickapoo River. Wealthy ginseng grower Charles Lord used his profits from peddling the exotic herb to the Oriental market to construct the place in 1908.

Rates are between $60 and $90 a night for two persons, which includes a five-course breakfast prepared by owner Pat Barnes. Ah, that oven-baked French toast! Inquire about bringing children. Four rooms available. The inn is near the entrance to the state park on Highway 33.

The Czechs and Bohemians celebrate their heritage in mid-June with an annual town festival. Polka-dancing fans come from miles around to flit around the dance pavilions. The active exercise is a requirement to get rid of pounds gained from nibbling rich Bohemian foods at the concession stands.

County seat Viroqua annually hosts the county fair on grounds on the north edge of town. Some of the best harness racing in the state can be seen at the September event. Drivers and breeders don't mind bragging when inquisitive visitors come around to see the stables and the animals.

There's a lot of competition in dairy classes as well. Watching the judging will help you learn the difference between a Holstein and a Guernsey. There's a lot of difference between one breed and an-udder.

Later in the month, usually on the last Saturday in September, nearby Viola (just 13 miles east of Viroqua on Highway 56) features a yearly horse and colt show. Get there by 9:30 A.M. to watch the pony and horse pulling contests. No, the spectators don't pull the horses. The teams are hitched to weighted sleds that are to be pulled a certain distance. A horse show usually begins at 9:00 A.M. and runs throughout the day. There's an afternoon parade, a dance at night, a tractor pull, midway rides, and exhibits by the Future Farmers of America and the 4-H. It's all real down-home.

The descendants of Norwegians, Czechs, and Bohemians make up a strong percentage of the Vernon County population. In fact, one of the largest clusters of Norwegians outside the Old Country lives in the stretch along Highway 14 between La Crosse and Westby. ◆**Norskedalen,** on County Road P at Coon Valley, is a refurbished pioneer homesite and a 350-acre arboretum along with nature trails.

The arboretum is a project of the University of Wisconsin–La Crosse to give students a firsthand look at the most up-to-date horticultural techniques. Tours are conducted by appointment, but drop-by visitors are always encouraged. Admission is $3.00 for adults and $2.00 for students kindergarten age through twelve. The Norwegian homestead is closed during the winter, but the grounds are open during the daylight hours.

The visitor's center is open year-round from 9:00 A.M. to 4:00 P.M. Saturdays and noon to 4:00 P.M. Sundays. From May 1 to October 31, the visitor's center on site is open from 9:00 A.M. to 4:30 P.M. Mondays through Saturdays and from noon to 4:30 P.M. Sundays.

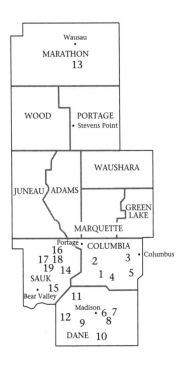

1. MacKenzie Environmental Center
2. Old Indian Agency House
3. National Watermelon Seed Spitting Contest
4. Leopold Memorial Reserve
5. Christopher Columbus Museum
6. Law Park
7. Art Fair off the Square
8. Capital Brewery and Beer Garden
9. Cave of the Mounds

10. Song of Norway Festival
11. Wollersheim Winery
12. Hoofbeat Ridge
13. Rib Mountain
14. Devil's Lake State Park
15. Merrimac ferryboat
16. Stand Rock Indian Ceremonial
17. Circus World Museum
18. Mid-Continent Railway Museum
19. Museum of Norman Rockwell Art

# CENTRAL WISCONSIN

Central Wisconsin is a rare mixture of tourism fun, urban bustle, political muscle, and natural beauty. It seems as if the best of what the state has to offer has come together here in a potpourri of sights and color.

There's the hustle and bustle of Dane County and Madison, the state capital, combined with the rural "outcountry" of Wisconsin's river heartland.

## COLUMBIA COUNTY

About 4 miles south of Arlington on Highway 51 is the University of Wisconsin Agricultural Research Station, an outdoor lab run by the University of Wisconsin. Researchers work on crop, livestock, and soil studies, and no one minds if you stop by for a quick visit. The farm on Hopkins Road (608–262–2996) is open all year from 8:00 A.M. to 4:30 P.M. Mondays through Fridays. If you need a goose to get you to Arlington, there are plenty to be had at the Goose Pond, so take Highway K west from town to Goose Pond Road.

Spring and fall migrations cover the marshland and nearby cornfields with great gaggles of geese. I've always wondered about how many pillows and quilts we could fill with all those fluttering feathers.

Four miles north of Arlington is the ◆ **MacKenzie Environmental Center** at Poynette, 1 mile east of town on Highway CS. The state Department of Natural Resources manages the center, which offers displays of native Wisconsin animals and has an interlocking network of excellent hiking trails. The center is open daily from 8:00 A.M. to 4:00 P.M. and is closed on winter holidays. Call (608) 635–4498 if you need more specifics.

Folks in Portage, the Columbia County seat, say this "is where the North begins." A trading post was established here in 1792, and enterpreneurs formed transport companies to aid commercial travel between the Fox and Wisconsin rivers. Oxen would tow empty barges across the connecting mud flats for $10. Fifty cents per one hundred pounds of merchandise was the going price for loaded vessels. A canal was eventually dug, linking the rivers and opening with much fanfare in 1851. Portage is home of the ◆ **Old Indian Agency House,** built in 1832 for agent John Kinzie and his wife, Juliet, a prolific writer. One of her works, *Waubun,* was a detailed account of her family's trip to Fort Winnebago that told as well about general pioneer life and their frontier home. Their granddaughter, Juliette Gordon Low, founded the Girl Scouts of the U.S.A.

The Kinzie house has been restored in the style of 1833 and is open for tours from May through mid-October (608–742–6362). Admission is $3.00 for adults, $1.00 for children, and $2.50 for seniors and AAA members. Hours are 10:00 A.M. to 4:00 P.M. daily throughout the year.

The house is opposite the site of the old fort, facing the canal built near the portage between the two rivers. The Fort Winnebago Surgeon's Quarters is the only remaining building in what was once an expansive complex of barracks, offices, and stores. Several well-known military men served at Fort Winnebago during its heyday. Their ranks included Jefferson Davis, then a young lieutenant, who went on to become president of the Confederacy during the Civil War.

Admission prices and tour hours are the same as at the Old Indian Agency House. The surgeon's quarters overlooks the site where French explorers Louis Joliet and Father Jacques Marquette beached their canoes in 1673 on the Fox River banks. Displays in the rough-looking building include period medical books, desks built by soldiers, an operating table, and the fort's records.

Anyone interested in building restorations should study the design of the place. Shaved pine logs squared off by axes form the outer walls. Tamarack poles make up the floor and ceiling joists. Much of the original plank flooring is still in place. The interior was plastered over handmade lathwork. The restorers left a portion uncovered so visitors can see the skill that went into making the building inhabitable.

The agency house and surgeon's quarters are 1.5 miles east of town on Highway 33.

Pardeeville, about 8 miles east of Portage on Highway 33 and 2 miles south on Highway 22, annually hosts the ◆ **National Watermelon Seed Spitting Contest** on the second Sunday in September. Admission is free, but come early. Competition in twelve different categories is always tough. Call (608) 429–2442 for details. Hope for a strong wind.

**35**

Across the river from Portage is the ❖ **Leopold Memorial Reserve** (608–356–9229), covering 1,300 acres of "sand country" loved by the famed naturalist Aldo Leopold. If you plan on visiting, read an excellent book on the outdoorsman's life by Curt Meine, entitled *Aldo Leopold: His Life and Work* (University of Wisconsin Press, 1988). In the 1930s and 1940s, Leopold wrote much of his famous *Sand County Almanac* in "The Shack," a converted chicken coop he used to get away from the rush and bustle of urban life. The spartan retreat is still on the reserve property, the nucleus of what is eighty acres that had been part of Leopold's riverbottom farm.

Columbus is proud to be named after the great Italian explorer and celebrated in grand style the 1992 anniversary of Columbus's landing in the New World. A sprawling ❖ **Christopher Columbus Museum** is packed with artifacts and memorabilia from the 1893 World's Columbian Exposition, which marked the 400th anniversary of the navigator's arrival in America.

The museum is on the top floor of the Columbus Antique Mall. The mall's 52,000 square feet make it the largest antique sales outlet in Wisconsin. "You name it, we have it. If it isn't here, you won't find it anywhere," claim the sales clerks. Owner Dan Amato purchased the three-story, tan brick former canning plant and opened the mall in 1983. Collecting the Columbus material started out as a hobby and then grew out of control. The mall and museum are open from 9:00 A.M. to 4:00 P.M. daily except Christmas. There's a $1.00 admission charge to the museum.

The building, at 239 Whitney Street (414–623–1992), is on the west side of the Crawfish River adjacent to the Columbus Water & Light Company.

## DANE COUNTY

The greater Madison area has been making a hit with visitors since noted nineteenth-century newspaper publisher Horace Greeley wrote, "Madison has the most magnificent site of any inland town I ever saw." That was in 1855, ten years after the community received the nod as capital of the state. Several generations later, the magic was still there. The old *Life* magazine took a closer look and proclaimed that the city's image best represented the "good life in America."

In 1978, the National Municipal League tagged Madison as an All-American City. Other studies have said that Madison is one of the most livable cities in the country. Of course, all the tourist and chamber of commerce promotions proudly toot their collective horns over the praise. But is it true? We think so. Besides, Madison's beaten paths are really a bit offbeat anyway, which makes everything in this town a delightful lark. Mad City is fine-tuned to the needs of citizens.

We like to think the lakes make the city something special. Mendota, Monona, Wingra, and Waubesa are within the city limits, comprising some 18,000 acres of watery surface on which to splash, puddle, paddle, or fish. Two sections of town are linked by an isthmus between Monona on the south and Mendota on the north, with the Capitol complex smack in the center.

You can get a free map of the lakes at bait shops in town. Speaking of free, the Capital City Ski Team presents delightfully nerve-wracking waterskiing shows at 7:00 P.M. Thursdays and Sundays from Memorial Day through Labor Day at ◈ **Law Park** on Lake Monona, a half mile southeast from Capitol Concourse. Get there early because the regulars stake out their grassy patch well before show time, bringing well-stocked coolers, Frisbees, and blankets. Don't forget mosquito repellent for July nights. The buzzers aren't as big as their North Woods cousins, but they can be as aggravating as lobbyists outside the assembly chambers at state budget time.

How can you beat a town that has 150 parks within the city limits, comprising some 3,600 acres of recreationland? In addition, Madison has one of the best places in the world to view a sunset: on the Memorial Union Terrace of the University of Wisconsin, overlooking Lake Mendota.

We have totaled up some other statistics for you, thanks to friends at *Isthmus* magazine who put out an "annual manual," as well as other knowledgeable Madison insiders. The city has 89 tennis courts, 22 touch football teams, 16 bathing beaches (13 staffed with lifeguards), 6 million volumes in the community's various libraries, 965 softball teams, 27 fine arts and performing theaters in addition to the 2,200-seat complex in the downtown Civic Center, 10 boat-launching sites ($2/day), and 5,016 parking meters. The excellent bus system is one of the best in the state for ease of transportation.

Biking is a relaxed way to see the city. According to confirmed pedalers who work for the Madison police department, there are three bikes to every car in the city, with some 98 miles of posted bike trails—perhaps that's because of the city's youthful makeup. Out of the total population of about 191,262 residents, 43,000 are university students, with two-thirds of the city's population when school is in session thirty-five years of age or under.

Bring your own bike to town or rent one at the **Budget Bicycle Center & Bicycle Rental,** 1202 Regent Street (608–251–8413), just five blocks from the U.W. Arboretum and near the Lake Mendota bike path.

One of the better trails is the loop around Lake Monona through Law Park, B. B. Clarke Park, and the fifty-one acres of the Olbrich Botanical Gardens. Give yourself at least a half day for that jaunt. Other good trails cover the scenic lakeshore from the university's Helen C. White Library to the apple trees at Picnic Point, Madison's best known locale for smooching, proposing marriage, and munching Oscar Mayer ring bologna on Ritz crackers (not necessarily in that order).

Walking is a good way to see Madison up close, too. Start in **Capitol Square,** more popularly called the Concourse. The Wisconsin Chamber Orchestra puts on free classical concerts there the last Wednesday of each June, every Wednesday in July, and the first Wednesday in August. On the first Saturday in June, kicking off the state's Dairy Month, you can milk a Holstein or a Guernsey cow on the Concourse. The bovines belong to the university, brought to the Capitol steps from the school farms on Campus Drive, a mile west of the Concourse (Madison has the honor of being the country's only major city with a working farm almost downtown).

Another agricultural tie is the farmers' market, which sets up camp on the Concourse from 6:00 A.M. to 2:00 P.M. each Saturday from May through autumn, and you can squeeze melons to your heart's content (in November and December, the market moves indoors to the Civic Center).

We make a practice out of hitting the Madison Art Fair on the weekend after July 4, a show that fills the Concourse with really respectable fine arts. What's most fun is watching the entertainers who ramble through the crowds. The Morris Dancers, who put on a traditional act dating to medieval England, are regulars, prancing around in their tattered clothes bedecked with ribbons. They expect donations after their routines, so be prepared to drop some change into the tin cups and old hats they pass around. Then there are the fire-eaters and jugglers, the balancing acts, the poetry readers, and the legislators shaking hands. Entertainers all.

Over the past few years, more restaurants have begun to provide varieties of food, getting away from the ordinary brat and hot dog review. The **Essen Haus un Trinken Halle,** 514 E. Wilson Street (608–255–4674), presents a German beer garden complete with polka bands. The **White Horse Inn,** 202 N. Henry Street (608–255–9933), sets a fabled salad bar.

On the same weekend, the ◆**Art Fair off the Square** in Olin Terrace Park, two blocks southeast of the Concourse, features tons of items in the craft vein. This alternative art fair also leans toward unconventional art, the more unusual—so turn your mind loose.

The Taste of Madison, on the Sunday of Labor Day weekend, brings fifty of the city's best restaurants to the Capitol Concourse. It's always fun to watch the waiters' race, an institution at the event. Dignitaries "love" the Gelatin Jump, into which they can leap for charity fund-raising.

Speaking of racing, enter the Mad City Marathon at the end of May. Whether crawling, walking, or running, the leg-stretching event is fun and great exercise for families and folks of any age. The loop extends around the city, starting on the south side of Lake Monona, then wends through downtown and neighborhoods to the north, through Maple Grove (wave to the governor, who comes out to stand on the front porch of the executive mansion there) and back down to Lake Wingra.

Take advantage of the free tours in the imposing Wisconsin Capitol building itself, built between 1907 and 1917. Kids like to find as many carved badgers as possible hidden in cornices, over stairwells, and elsewhere.

The outside dome is topped by a gold-leafed statue officially known as "Wisconsin," artist Daniel Chester French's rendition of what he thought the image of the state should be. No, it isn't a dairy cow, but a toga-draped woman of indeterminate age who has a badger on her head! The best place to view this dauntless lady, other than by helicopter, is from the eighth floor Top of the Park restaurant of the Inn on the Park hotel, 22 S. Carroll Street

(608–257–8811). The restaurant windows are across the street from the Capitol Concourse to the west. The food is worth the view, but the place is a bit pricey.

But back to the Capitol, an occasional old haunt when I was a reporter with the *Milwaukee Sentinel*. In those days, I was dedicated to chasing politicians and bureaucrats through the labyrinth of hallways in pursuit of truth, justice, and a front-page byline. I learned that some of the byways in the building were more interesting than the politicos. A favorite place was, and still is, the **Grand Army of the Republic Memorial Hall** honoring the 83,400 Wisconsonites who served in the Union Army during the Civil War.

The state sent fifty-three infantry regiments, four cavalry units, and one battalion of heavy artillery into the conflict's smoke and fire, as part of the famed Iron Brigade. Of the total, 11,000 of the men never returned, dying of wounds or disease. Their regimental battle flags are on display in the fourth-floor hall, along with other memorabilia.

The displays are open to the public from 9:00 A.M. to 4:30 P.M. weekdays year-round and during the same hours on weekends as well from Memorial Day to Labor Day.

After strolling around the Concourse, hit State Street. In Madison, that's the avenue to see and be seen. It's lined with oddball shops where you can purchase 1930s ball gowns or mountaineering gear, scuba equipment or fish sandwiches, books or crystals. The street is home to the **Madison Civic Center and Gallery,** a couple of theaters, hot singles bars, and the city's trendier restaurants. We won't discuss the last because they tend to come and go. But you'll generally do all right at any of them. Don't simply look at ground level, either. Many of the eateries are on second floors, with banks of windows overlooking the parade below. **Ella's Deli,** a Madison institution for more than a generation, is located at 425 State Street. Ella's is an old-fashioned kosher deli with all the corned beef and bagel trimmings. Try their hot fudge sundaes for complete degradation.

The eclectic crowd on the street is a mixture of bustling government workers, intent university students, high school kids trying to look cool, bearded street musicians, tourists, and middle-class shoppers.

Williamson Street, better known as Willy Street, is Madison's hip avenue running along the Lake Monona shoreline, with its range of services from a tattoo parlor to a community health clinic. At the mouth of Willy Street is the Gateway building, a strip mall of ten stores making a neat welcome to the street. The merchants and residents in the neighborhood sponsor a great street fair in mid-September.

Nearby is the local food co-op (1202 Williamson, 608–251–6776) for getting last-minute coffee in bulk, fresh avocados, or health foods. The **Duerst New and Used Variety Store,** 1236 Williamson, is unique. Shoppers there can get mattresses on sale or vacuum cleaners fixed. If that's not enough, the proprietor is also a faith healer who takes appointments as well as drop-in emergencies.

For pampering of another sort, the **Mansion Hill Inn** is Madison's ultimate in style. The building on 424 N. Pinckney Street was constructed in 1858 by the tradesman who built Madison's second capitol building. It went through a succession of owners and housed students during its declining years. The place was purchased by Randy Alexander, a young rehabilitation specialist who had resurrected other fading Madison homes and buildings. He returned the mansion to its former elegance, a veritable posh palace. Alexander brought in his army of craftworkers who spent a year patching, plastering, and painting the place. The antique-filled rooms are comfortable and cozy, especially when you're coming in from a fog-bound, late-winter day. Each bathroom has been snazzed up by Kohler Corporation (Wisconsin-made!) bath devices that bubble, whirl, and refresh the most battered bod.

Other pluses: A valet parks your car; another serves coffee by the downstairs fireplace. As such, Mansion Hill has become the "in place" for executives and visiting government types who appreciate little touches.

Honeymooners enjoy the Mansion as well. They probably don't pay much attention, but the telephones have computer modem hookups and teleconference connections. But they probably appreciate the two Rolls-Royces available for hire there, if someone needs to run out quickly for extra champagne. Call (608) 255–3999 for reservations.

Other must-see places in Madison:

The **Credit Union National Association,** 5810 Mineral Point Road (608–231–4000), has an interesting museum that traces the history of economics and coinage, leading to the formation of credit unions. The complex at the corner of Mineral Point and Rosa roads is also home for the World Council of Credit Unions, with 60 million members. The museum is open during weekly business hours.

The **Elvehjem Museum of Art,** 800 University Avenue (608–263–2246)—pronounced "L-V-M" for a passable Scandinavian accent—is one of the better places in town. But you have to check the traveling exhibits as well as the 10,000 pieces in the permanent collection. The gallery is open from 9:00 A.M. to 4:45 P.M. daily.

Don't you dare miss **Babcock Hall** at the University of Wisconsin-Madison. "Ice cream, ice cream, we all scream for ice cream" is the anthem at Babcock, the university's dairy science building, on 1605 Linden Drive.

From the Capitol Concourse, drive west on University Avenue and take the campus exit near the university greenhouses (which look like greenhouses) to Linden, the first left at the four-way stop. Babcock will be immediately on the left by the Stock Pavilion, an export center for horse shows and other agricultural events.

The university's own contented cows and friendly Dane County farmers provide the base product for the whole, 2 percent, and skim milk, buttermilk, cheese, and yogurt produced there. Yet ice cream is the best-seller in the Babcock Hall retail store, the Memorial Union, and Union South. Cones and sundaes are available in the two union buildings, while quarts and gallons can be purchased in Babcock Hall. The university's dorm food service also offers the dairy goods for the cafeteria lines.

The ice cream is 12 percent butterfat, rather than the industry standard of only 10 percent, according to the plant directors. Pure cane sugar instead of corn sweeteners is used. With Babcock ice cream, you'll never get just a cone full of air, as with some other commercial preparations.

Warner Park is longtime home of the Madison Muskies, the city's semiprofessional baseball team, where the boys of summer smack base hits and snag flies. The promotion-minded team offers regular Muskieteer Days for youngsters under age fourteen who belong to its Muskieteers Club; they get free admission to Sunday games. Fifty-cent plump ballpark hot dogs are offered on Monday, with Baseball Bingo Night on Friday. Families get in for $5.00 on Thursday nights to roar their encouragement as the locals battle the Appleton Foxes and the Beloit Brewers, among the state's other clubs. There's hardly a better way to spend a traditional hot August evening.

Some helpful Madison contacts follow:

• Parks Department, Madison Municipal Building, Suite 120, 215 Martin Luther King Jr. Boulevard, Madison 53710 (608–266–4711). The street name was changed from Monona Avenue in 1987.

• Greater Madison Convention and Visitors Bureau, 615 E. Washington Avenue, Madison 53703 (608–255–2537 or 25–LAKES). A twenty-four-hour answering service can take messages or record a request for an information packet. Just leave a name and address.

• *Isthmus* magazine (free on newsstands; $25.00 annual subscription fee), 14 W. Mifflin Street, Madison 53703 (608–251–5627). The magazine does the best job reporting on entertainment and events on a weekly basis, coming out on Thursdays.

Michael Feldman, whose goofy and often irreverent commentary has catapulted his "Whadya Know" radio program into National Public Radio syndication, holds sway on Saturday mornings. Seating for the program is at 9:00 A.M., with the live airing at 10:00 A.M. Feldman offers a potpourri of silly quizzes, with contestants plucked from the audience and from among callers around the nation. This is a chance to be a broadcast star! Show up at the Parliamentary Room in Vilas Hall of the University of Wisconsin-Madison, and don't be bashful if a mike is suddenly thrust in front of you.

Middleton, Madison's closest western suburb, is home of the ✦ **Capital Brewery and Beer Garden,** on 7734 Terrace, one of the state's newest breweries. Weather permitting, the beer garden here is a great place to loll away a summer Saturday afternoon. This microbrewery makes a smooth GartenBrau in light, dark, and seasonal draughts. Tours are run several times a day, usually when there's a big enough crowd. Brewmaster Kirby Nelson pours mean brews while he chats about malts and barleys.

Middleton is also home of **Clasen's European Bakery,** 2910 Laura Lane (608–831–6750), probably one of the state's *best* bakeries. The company is owned by Ernest and Rolf Clasen, who immigrated from Gerolstein, Germany, in the late 1950s. Both are *konditors,* officially recognized pastry chefs. They emphatically state they are NOT just bakers. For a time, the brothers made only candy.

When the price of sugar skyrocketed in the 1960s, they moved into tortes and coffee cakes, although a major portion of their business remains manufacturing chocolate that is shipped out by the semitrailer-truckload and in fifty-pound wafers. But, oh, those baked items. In the rear self-service room, banks of refrigeration units house towering cream cakes. Trays are laden with breads and cookies. Just remembering a recent stop adds pounds where they shouldn't be. Shop hours are 8:00 A.M. to 5:00 P.M. Mondays through Saturdays.

The **Old Middleton Centre** offers a variety of gift shops and boutiques. The outdoor gazebo in the center of the complex, located at 750 Hubbard Avenue (608–836–6896), is a good place to relax and rest your feet after shopping. The Centre is three blocks northeast of the Capital Brewery. From Terrace Avenue East, take the first left (Hubbard), then go two blocks, and the shops will be on your left. The Centre is considered one of the best places in the Madison area for purchasing smaller imported gift items such as plates and crystal.

For eating in Middleton, try the **Gallery,** 1904 Parmenter Street, (608–831–5000). The restaurant and lounge has as much foliage and running water as an exotic veranda in Sri Lanka. But it's not so overdone you need a machete to find the menu. Try the swordfish (ask for it grilled) for a Wisconsin taste treat. And, to answer the obvious question, no, swordfish is not native to the state. Prices are moderate.

◆ **Cave of the Mounds** in Blue Mounds is only 20 miles west of Madison on Highways 18 and 151. The caves have the usual selection of stalagmites, stalactites, and pools that make a great several-hour stopover for anyone with a carful of kids. The history of the place is the most interesting, however. The farm on which the caves were discovered date from 1828 and is one of the oldest in Dane County. In December 1987, Cave of the Mounds was designated a national natural landmark by the Department of the Interior. Tickets to Cave of the Mounds cost $7.00 for adults, $6.00 for seniors, and $3.00 for kids ages five to twelve. Hours are 9:00 A.M. to 5:00 P.M. weekends from November 15 to March 15 and 9:00 A.M. to 7:00 P.M. daily from Memorial Day to Labor Day. Tours take about forty-five minutes, kicked off by a slide show. A self-guided nature trail over seven acres of the farm is also available. Although there's a

**Cave of the Mounds**

restaurant on the premises, the cave owners don't mind if guests bring picnic lunches. They've provided a pleasantly shaded grove for snacking. For more details, contact Cave of the Mounds (608–437–3038).

"Velkommen" is the greeting in Mount Horeb, one of several Norwegian communities at the western edge of Dane County. Although the town was originally settled by English, Irish, and German settlers in 1861, three-quarters of the population was Scandinavian by 1870. Since there is one-quarter Larson in our blood, we occasionally like to stop and find out the latest on the Norskie front. The folks there annually put on a six-week mid-summer program called the ❖ **Song of Norway Festival,** which culminates in the presentation of the musical comedy *Song of Norway.*

The play is loosely based on the life of Norwegian composer Edvard Grieg. The show is usually offered the last Saturday in June and each Saturday in July. For times and ticket prices, contact the Mount Horeb Chamber of Commerce, Mount Horeb 53572.

You'll know this is the right town by the giant trolls lurking outside the **Open House Imports,** 308 E. Main Street, one of several excellent import and gift shops. The trolls are statues, of course, yet when our kids were younger they were never quite sure. Since trolls turn to stone in the daylight, they had a sneaking suspicion that there might have once been such live creatures.

Other attractions in the Mount Horeb area include the **Tyrol Ski Basin, Blue Mounds State Park,** and **Little Norway,** a Norwegian pioneer homesite and church.

The only Wisconsin winery on the National Register of Historic Places is the ❖ **Wollersheim Winery,** on Highway 188, a quarter mile south of Highway 60. Just across the Wisconsin River is the village of Prairie du Sac. The original vineyards were planted in the 1840s by Count Agoston Haraszthy, a Hungarian whose dreams exceeded the reality of Wisconsin's harsh winters. The noble became discouraged after several years of cold, so he eventually sold out, moved to California to help establish the wine industry there, and subsequently made his fortune. The new owner was Peter Kehl, whose family were vintners since 1533 in Germany's Rhineland.

Kehl built most of the complex's existing buildings, operating the winery until a killing frost in 1899 effectively destroyed the crop. After a generation of vacancy, the grounds were purchased in 1972 by Bob and JoAnn Wollersheim. They replanted the slopes with such hearty hybrids as Millot, De Chaunac, and Foch for red wines and Aurora and Seyval Blanc for white wines.

Winemaker Phillipe Coquard, whose family is in the wine business in the Beaujolais region of France, is especially proud of the ruby nouveau produced each autumn. This young wine has beaten out competitors from Oregon, California, New York, and other wine-growing states in major competitions.

In 1990 the Wollersheims purchased the old Stone Mill Winery in Cedarburg (Ozaukee County). Renamed the Cedar Creek Winery, that facility has also started winning its share of awards.

Winery tours can be taken between 10:00 A.M. and 5:00 P.M. daily year-round, followed by a wine tasting, of course. Throughout the year, the Wollersheims do more than just show off their kegs and casks of award-winning wine. As great promoters, they sponsor numerous programs, ranging from a spring folk festival, grape-growing seminars, wine-making instructions, and a harvest festival that features a grape-stomping contest. For specific dates, contact the Wollersheims at their winery (608–643–6515).

If you come to the area in winter, bald eagles can occasionally be seen swooping high over the snow-covered cornfields. The huge birds dive for fish on the Wisconsin River, with the best opportunities for spotting the eagles being in the vicinity of the Prairie du Sac dam.

The recently established **Wisconsin Folk Museum** swung open its doors in early 1991, featuring wood carvings, whirligigs, quilts, and dozens of other items highlighting the state's heritage. The museum is located at 100 S. Second Street in downtown Mount Horeb, twenty minutes west of Madison.

One of the most interesting displays is a large hand-whittled American flag, dating from the 1930s. Phil Martin, museum director, says the stars on the flag's blue field are carved from a single block of wood. The stripes are whittled chains, some of which are 5 feet long. It's quite a sight. Call (608) 437–4742 for more information.

Mazomanie is located along Reeve Road off Highway 14. The town name was taken from the Sauk Indian term loosely translated as "Iron Horse" or "Iron that Walks," referring to the old-time trains that rumbled through here during the pioneer era. Take Reeve Road on the west end of town to ◆**Hoofbeat Ridge,** an accredited American Camping Association horseback riding camp that offers numerous weekend and special events in addition to its regular camp and riding lesson schedules. The camp has been operated by the Bennett family (founders John and Betty Bennett had eleven kids!) and assorted in-laws since 1963. It's one of the largest horse camps in Wisconsin, with strict adherence to safety and promoting the understanding of what horses are all about. Both western and English styles of riding are taught. All our kids have attended several years of summer camp at Hoofbeat and subsequently have become competent, careful riders. What makes Hoofbeat special are the adult riding weekends, family camp-outs, riding shows, dressage presentations, and similar programs beyond the regularly scheduled riding classes and summer camp. Remember, this is a casual place, one for blue jeans and boots, but highly professional in its approach to teaching folks how to ride properly and well.

During the winter, cross-country skiing is popular on the riding trails. For details, contact Director Ted Marthe, Hoofbeat Ridge Camp, 5304 Reeve Road, Mazomanie 53560 (608–767–2593).

To the southeast of Madison on Highway 18 is the small community of Cambridge, home to several pottery works. **Rockdale Union Stoneware,** 137 W. Main Street (608–423–4843), and **Rowe Pottery,** with its outlet store on 404 England Street, have broad selections of saltglaze pottery in gray and blue hues. Rowe's plant is in Rock County's Edgerton (608–884–9483).

This farming community is at the western edge of Wisconsin's major tobacco-growing area. Along the highway are farms with their distinctive open-sided barns, used for drying the tobacco leaves. This Wisconsin product is generally used for cigar wrappings.

Famed artist Georgia O'Keeffe is remembered around her home community of Sun Prairie, a rural community about 7 miles northeast of Madison. She was born on a farm 3.5 miles southeast of town on November 15, 1887. A red roadside plaque now marks the spot. When she was fourteen, she moved away with her family to Virginia and went on to pursue her meteoric career in the American Southwest. An autographed copy of one of her catalogs and one of her works are displayed at the **Sun Prairie Library and Museum** on Main Street. A meeting room in the library, where the town council meets, was dedicated to O'Keeffe in 1987, the year after her death.

The dramatic power of the Ice Age is readily evident throughout this part of the state, especially in the Devil's Lake area and the Baraboo Range. This stretch of jagged limestone cliffs, moraine deposits, and deep valleys lies about 3 miles south of Baraboo and 20 miles south of the Wisconsin Dells. Wisconsin Highways 159, 123, 113, and 33 enter the area of gorges, hills, crests, flatlands, and river bottoms. Access to the state roads is easy via Interstates 90/94, with interchanges some 12 miles east and north of Devil's Lake. Highway 12 cuts straight south from the Dells to the Wisconsin River, crossing at Sauk City and on into Madison.

That highway must have more roadhouses per mile than any other stretch in the state. A roadhouse, as you know, might have a wild and woolly history comprised of equal parts bathtub gin, flappers, and who knows what else.

Wisconsin roadhouses these days are calmer, of course, but you can drop by for a shot and a beer, a sandwich, and some great local conversation tossed in for good measure. The Missouri Tavern, Ma Schmitty's, Charlie Brown's, the Springfield Inn, and others along Highway 12, between Highway 19 and Madison, might appear to be diamonds in the rough. But give 'em a try—you'll generally like what you find. They are especially cozy on a blizzardy Wisconsin afternoon, before the plows arrive to beat back the drifts creeping in across the fields.

## MARATHON COUNTY

The sprawling paper factories of Wausau pale in significance when compared to ◆ **Rib Mountain,** the billion-year-old hunk of rock that towers above the city on its west side. The mountain, complete with a state park campground, mountain biking, and ski runs, was not crunched by the glaciers that flattened the rest of Wisconsin 10,000 years ago. The mountain is 1,940 feet high, the second-highest peak in the state, providing plenty of recreational opportunities for the active-minded. Just to the south of Rib Mountain is the county's **Nine-Mile Recreation Area** on Red Bud Road off County Highway N, a labyrinth of backroads and logging paths that are available for cross-country skiing and more biking.

For a more urbane experience, Wausau's Artrageous Weekend in September takes over the downtown pedestrian mall, where artists and craftworkers display their wares. In addition to wandering musicians, jugglers, and other street performers, there is a children's hands-on area where they paint and learn to make pottery.

Just south of Wausau on Highway S is the 20,000-acre **George W. Meade Wildlife Area** (715–848–6143), one of the best picnic areas in the state. It's also a good location for deer and duck watching.

## SAUK COUNTY

According to archaeologists, the ancient Wisconsin River cut an 800-foot-deep trench through this vicinity in the eons before the Ice Age. When the latest push by glaciers moved southward in several waves (70,000 to 10,000 years ago), ice from the so-called Green Bay glacial lobe spread its cold fingers around the hills comprising today's rocky Baraboo Range. Both ends of the river gorge were plugged with ice, which created the Devil's Lake basin. Eventually, the ice melted and dumped millions of tons of debris into the riverbed, pushing the river itself about 9 miles to the east, where it is today.

Subsequently, softened by expansive stands of oak and birch groves, the resulting landscape with all its bumps and dips is considered some of the most beautiful scenery in the state. The centerpiece is the 5,100-acre ◆**Devil's Lake State Park,** which attracts more than 1.5 million visitors a year.

The park offers 450 campsites, hiking trails, swimming, fishing, and sailing. Since the place is so expansive, you can generally rummage around to your heart's content without rubbing shoulders with anyone else.

The busiest days, however, are those bustling June, July, and August weekends when the campgrounds are generally booked and the lake banks seem knee-deep in kids with plastic fishing rods.

But don't let that keep you away at other times. Midweek and off-season visits leave plenty of room to ramble. Since the state park is central to the tourist attractions in the Dells, the Madison scene, and other getaways in the vicinity, it makes for a good jumping-off point if your family is in the camping mood.

The second major physical feature of central Wisconsin is the mighty Wisconsin River, which bisects the state. It's the longest river in Wisconsin, easily earning the same name. The waterway runs some 430 miles from the lake district in northeastern

Wisconsin to the Mississippi River at Prairie du Chien. At Portage, the Wisconsin connects to the Fox River, which in turn eventually links up with Lake Michigan.

These days, the tannin-colored river is a favorite for canoeists and anglers. In early years, the river was a major route for the massive lumber rafts floated downstream to the sawmills. Today, sunbathers, looking like bratwurst on a grill as they loll about during hot summer afternoons, enjoy the seclusion of dunes and sandbars along the riverbanks.

Over the past few years, several of the more remote stretches of beach frontage have been taken over by nudists, many of them college students from the University of Wisconsin in nearby Madison. More than one canoeing party has been surprised by tanned (or brightly sunburned pink) folks in the buff who wave friendly greetings. For decorum's sake, we won't tell you the exact sandbars . . . but . . . if you put your canoe in the river at the Highway 14 crossing, across from Helena and Tower Hill campground . . .

A more staid way to make the river crossing is via the ♦ **Merrimac ferryboat.** Since the Wisconsin Department of Transportation gained control of passage over the Wisconsin River in 1933, motorists, hikers, and bikers have been getting a free ride. The first ferry was operating at the same site as early as 1844. Currently, the *Colsac II* runs twenty-fours hours a day between April 15 and December 1, depending on winter ice conditions. Colsac stands for Columbia and Sauk counties, linked by the ferry. The ten-minute ride accommodates twelve cars or trucks each run; the ferry makes some 40,000 trips a season while carrying 195,000 vehicles. The crossing is reached via Highway 113 between Okee on the south shore and Merrimac on the north. The Wisconsin River is a half mile wide at this point, but the crossing saves a 9-mile drive west or a 12-mile drive east to the closest bridges.

Impress your kids by telling them that an underwater cable links the boat to shore, with the vessel's monster diesel engine pulling the boat and its load back and forth. The tykes will think you're a veritable maritime encyclopedia.

Rest rooms and privately run refreshment stands are conveniently located on each shore. Yet a warning is necessary. Don't get boxed between other waiting cars if the kids have to make a last-minute panic pit stop prior to boarding. It's difficult to pull out of line to retrieve a pokey youngster still in the facilities. The child may have to pick up the next ride over if you get carried away in the flow of traffic onto the ferry deck.

The centrally located Wisconsin Dells, touching Juneau, Adams, Sauk, and Columbia counties, is the epitome of what outsiders consider summer fun in Wisconsin. Visitors are drawn from around the Midwest to see the fudge shops, arcades, wax museums, shooting galleries, souvenir shops, and hamburger joints that line the streets of the Dells and the adjacent town of Lake Delton. Tourism is nothing new in the Dells neighborhood. Before the turn of the century, thousands of visitors flocked here to cruise the upper and lower sections of the Wisconsin River and marvel at the scenery. That remains the best part of a vacation in the region. There's little that can beat a river ride upstream on a warm summer day, with the chance to put your feet up on a rail and to admire the passing river bluffs.

It seems as if every high promontory has an Indian maiden leaping to her death because her lover died in battle or some other legend. The Dells also has such a cliff.

For the real thing, however, Native Americans have long been an integral part of the Dells tourism scene. The ◆ **Stand Rock Indian Ceremonial** is a pageant that has been performed at the Stand Rock Amphitheater since 1929. The best way to get there is via the river aboard an evening boat, which docks at a landing below the stage. The amphitheater is accessible by auto, but I still vote for boat. The tour vessel departs at 7:45 P.M. from the Dells landing downtown, leaving plenty of time for a pleasant evening cruise and the 8:45 P.M. show that runs through the summer season.

I've always thought the Upper Dells were more scenic than the section below the town. But you can make that choice for yourself. An exciting way to see the flowage is a ride on the Ducks, surplus World War II amphibious vehicles that bump and leap over set trails, splash through the Wisconsin River, and rumble along pathways near the town streets—much to the delight of riders. Keep your camera bags and purses off the floor because the splashing water often swirls along the base of the vehicle and out the back. Several companies offer rides.

The crown prince of the Wisconsin Dells is probably Tommy Bartlett, the impresario of a water, sky, and thrill show that has been a staple of Dells entertainment for three decades. Bartlett, who looks like Santa Claus on vacation, has packaged a great program of divers, splashers, fliers, and clowns for a show that runs several times daily throughout the season. It's a rain-or-shine proposition, so dress accordingly. Ask for the reserved seats, which are actually comfortable lawn chairs.

Attached to his water show park is **Robot World,** Bartlett's vision of a futuristic home operated by mechanical people. It's a worthwhile stop, with just the right tongue-in-cheek combination of hokeyness and fun. The lower level of the building is a hands-on science hall, where kids and adults can conduct all sorts of interesting physics experiments. You can often find Bartlett down there, having a good time along with his visitors. This place is a boon on a rainy day if you are traveling with youngsters. They'll have plenty to do. But get there early—other parents often have the same idea.

Some other rewarding stops in the neighborhood are the **Haunted Mansion, Storybook Gardens,** and **Noah's Ark Waterslide.** The old Wax Museum on Broadway in the Dells received a face-lift in 1988, changing its name to the **Wax World of Stars.** The revamped interior features glitzy Hollywood sets. An excellent attraction for photography fans is **Bennett House,** home of noted photographer Henry Hamilton Bennett, a nineteenth-century photographer who concentrated on the rocky Dells landscape for his scenes. You can compare his photos of early Dells tourism to today's lifestyles. There isn't that much difference, other than clothing and hair arrangements.

For comprehensive listings of prices, accommodations, and attractions, contact the Wisconsin Dells Visitor & Convention Bureau, 115 Wisconsin Avenue, Wisconsin Dells 53965 (608–254–4321); in Wisconsin, call toll-free (800) 223–3557; from neighboring states, call (800) 356–6611.

Our favorite place in Sauk County is Baraboo, old home of the Ringling Brothers Circus. Wisconsin is known as "The Mother of the Circus" because more than one hundred shows were organized here from pre–Civil War days to the 1980s. Baraboo is subsequently the High Seat of Circusdom in Wisconsin. The town is gung-ho show biz all the way, calling itself the Circus City of the Nation.

August Ringling, father of the famed circus family, operated harness shops in Baraboo after moving there from Prairie du

Chien in the mid-1800s. The Ringling boys loved entertainment life and began their Greatest Show on Earth (it wasn't quite that yet) in 1884. They winter-quartered along the Baraboo River (some folks still claim that an elephant or two was buried along the banks). Their cousins, the Gollmars, also operated a circus out of Baraboo, and numerous city residents were employed in wagon and harness making for the shows. Entertainers built homes in town, with practice barns and halls in their backyards. The friezes around the Courthouse Annex depict this delightful history.

The showpiece of Baraboo is the refurbished ◆ **Circus World Museum,** site of the old Ringling headquarters. In 1987 the CWM received a Phoenix Award from the Society of American Travel Writers for its preservation efforts. The museum's buildings and tents house the world's largest collection of rebuilt circus wagons and show off an extensive display of memorabilia, in addition to housing a vast research collection of posters, photos, route books, diaries, and similar artifacts. Wagons from the museum are shown each July in the Great Circus Parade in Milwaukee, hauled there by steam train. Being a circus nut myself, I've been coming to the CWM since the early 1960s, when the place opened. For the past few years, a selection of my own circus photos has been displayed there. They were taken while I was a correspondent for *Amusement Business* magazine, the national entertainment publication.

Take the CWM tour of town, on regularly dispatched trolleys from the museum entrance. You'll see the **Al Ringling Theater,** the harness shop owned by the Ringlings' father, and numerous houses in which circus performers lived. Live performances, including loading and unloading a circus train, are part of the show back on the grounds. Kids love getting their photos taken in the gorilla wagon near the front entrance. I've seen more than one teacher or guide glad to "lock up" a few wild tykes, even if only for a few minutes. The museum, operated by the State Historical Society, is located at 426 Water Street (608–356–8341).

Five miles north of Baraboo, just off Highway 12 on Shady Lane Road, is the **International Crane Foundation,** where you can see several species of cranes from around the world. From May until the end of October, the conservation group that runs the center is always happy to have visitors. Tours start at 10:00 A.M., 1:00 P.M., and 3:00 P.M., Memorial Day through Labor Day. Cost is $5.00 for adults, $4.50 for seniors, $2.50 for children ages five through twelve, and free for kids under five. Call first because of the mating and hatching season (608–356–9462). During that time, the curators often have to perform crane mating dances to get the big birds in the appropriate frame of mind. Now *that* makes for quite a sight, although the ritual is closed to the public.

North Freedom is home of the ◆**Mid-Continent Railway Museum,** operated by volunteers who love oil cans, iron, steam, and old trains. There are some 300 members of the Mid-Continent Railway Historical Society who have restored dozens of ancient engines and railcars, offering rides on a regular basis in the summer and autumn.

The D&R No. 9, built in 1884, is one of the country's oldest operating locomotives, repaired by society members in a huge car barn on their property. The "clubhouse" is a depot built in 1894, which houses exhibitions of equipment and railroad mementoes. I've always enjoyed the autumn color tours that the club sponsors on weekends when the leaves are reaching their maximum rainbow effect. Occasionally, at a particularly scenic curve, the train stops to allow photographers to get off and take pictures from near the tracks. The train will back up and make a steamy, roaring run past the clicking shutters to magnificent effect. And, yes, the train does return to pick everyone up.

The winter snow run during the third week in February is also great for photographs, but dress warmly. The coaches are heated by wood stoves, just as they would be in the old days. Those closest to the stove almost bake while the poor riders in the rear can get preeeettty frosty by the time the jaunt is completed. When getting off the train for those extra-special winter weather photos of a steam locomotive in action, be sure to wear appropriate foot coverings because snow along the tracks can be quite deep.

During the summer, the fifty-minute tour travels over its own railbed between the hills and valleys of the Baraboo Range from North Freedom to Quartzite Lake, stopping at the iron mining town of La Rue. Now a ghost town, the once-bustling community was served by the railroad in 1903.

Trains usually begin rolling toward mid-May, keeping up the action through Labor Day and some weekends through mid-October. Rides are scheduled for 10:30 A.M. and 12:30, 2:00, and

**D&R No. 9, Mid–Continent Railway Museum**

3:30 P.M. daily during the season. The museum is open from 9:30 A.M. until 5:00 P.M. Admission prices for adults are $7.00, children three to fifteen are $4.00, and senior citizens are $6.00. A family fare (two adults and two children) is $22.

Some of the historical society members live on the grounds all summer, sleeping in their private rail coaches for the ultimate in luxury. The care that they have put into repairing the venerable gear is worth a stop, since much of the rolling stock has been featured in commercials and movies. It's like watching someone you know appear in a starring role. Equipment from the museum has been featured in the Swedish film *The Emigrants* and in the movie, *Gaily, Gaily,* among numerous others.

North Freedom is reached by taking Interstate 90 to the Baraboo exit and going through Baraboo on Wisconsin Highway 33 to Wisconsin 136, where you can then follow the signs on County Road PF to the depot staging area. The complex is 6 miles west of Baraboo and 50 miles northwest of the Wisconsin Dells. For information on the Mid-Continent Railway Historical Society, contact the organization at Walnut Street, North Freedom 53951 (608–522–4261).

From Baraboo, head west again on Highway 136 to Highway 33 about 12 miles to Reedsburg and the **Museum of Norman Rockwell Art.** Curator Joyce Devore opened the exhibit featuring the famed commercial artist in an old church she purchased and refurbished in 1982. The museum, at 227 S. Park Street (608–524–2123), houses about 4,000 postcards, original magazine covers, calendars, and similar items on original paper stock painted by the famed illustrator between 1911 and 1976.

Devore is always seeking more material for displays but admits the pickings are getting slim these days. She has just about everything Rockwell ever completed but could use more vintage covers from *Boys' Life* magazines. Admission is $4.00 for adults and $3.00 for American Automobile Association members. Kids under age five are admitted free. The museum is open daily from 9:30 A.M. to 5:00 P.M., May through October, and from 11:00 A.M. to 5:00 P.M. Wednesdays to Saturdays in the winter.

On a more mundane note, the state Cow Chip Throwing Contest is jointly sponsored by Prairie du Sac and Sauk City, usually on the Saturday of Labor Day Weekend.

A cow chip is, well . . . see for yourself. The adjoining communities are along the Wisconsin River in the southern part of Sauk County. Call (608) 643–4663 for the details.

## WOOD COUNTY

Wisconsin Rapids has been a papermaking hub since the 1830s. Consolidated Papers, 231 First Avenue North (715–422–3111), offers tours of its plant and self-guided walks in nearby forestland owned by the firm.

# NORTHERN WISCONSIN

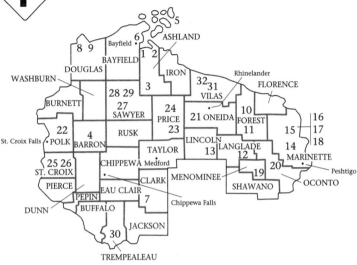

1. The Depot
2. Bad River Chippewa Reservation
3. Chequamegon National Forest
4. Rutabaga Festival
5. Apostle Islands Cruise Service
6. Big Top Chautauqua
7. HighGround Veterans Memorial Park
8. SS *Meteor*
9. Amnicon Falls State Park
10. Nicolet National Forest
11. Great Northern Bluegrass Festival
12. Wolf River Lodge
13. Merrill
14. Peshtigo Fire Museum
15. High Falls Dam
16. Twelve Foot Falls
17. Dave's Falls
18. American Outdoor Learning Center
19. Menominee Indian Reservation
20. Copper Culture Mound State Park
21. Rhinelander Logging Museum
22. Ice Age Interpretive Center
23. Timm's Hill
24. Wisconsin Concrete Park
25. Octagon House
26. Apple River
27. The Hideout
28. National Fresh Water Fishing Hall of Fame
29. Lumberjack World Championships
30. Lock and Dam No. 6
31. Baertschy's Colonial House
32. Vilas County Historical Museum

# Northern Wisconsin

There is a hoary joke they tell in the far reaches of Wisconsin whenever an Alberta Hook weather system swings down from Canada across Lake Superior to slam a wintry punch at the state. Amid the hail, frozen rain, and snow, the lament goes up, "I'm gonna put a snow shovel on my shoulder and walk south, stopping when the first person says," 'What's that you're carrying?'"

As an example of snow conditions, Bayfield County's Iron River recorded 32¾ inches of snow in January 1988, concluding a three-month fall of 64½ inches.

Some folks do abandon Wisconsin, thinking that less frosty winters will be a panacea to wintertime woes. Most people along the upper rim of the Badger State, however, take their seasons in stride. What are a few nasty February days when considering long summers in the pine woods, the excitement of snowmobiling and skiing in the winter, with the fresh explosion of spring wildflowers and the hazy crimson woods of autumn. These delights of Wisconsin ensure that its residents remain hardy and open to life around them.

And there are plenty of nooks and crannies that need exploring in northern Wisconsin.

## Ashland County

The city of Ashland calls itself the Garland City of the Inland Seas. That's a pretty hefty title, but since the community celebrated its centennial in 1987 we should allow them some imagery excess. Stepping back farther into history, French trappers and traders stopped by here regularly as early as 1659. Where the French used canoes to skirt the shoreline because the timber was so thick on shore, today's travelers can easily drive to **Sunset Recreational Vehicle Park** and gaze on the wind-ruffled waters of Chequamegon Bay. Payment is by the honor system.

A century ago, passenger and freight trains made Ashland a major transportation hub in the North Woods. With the demise of passenger trains, Ashland's Soo Line station crumbled. The wreck was a challenge to developer Mike Ryan, a former airline traffic manager who dabbled in refurbishing old buildings. At first, renovating the depot was a task that made him wonder about this avocation. Then he looked beyond the piles of rubble and the gaping hole in the roof and decided it wasn't so bad after all. After taking about sixty truckloads of trash and wreckage from the shell, Ryan saved the depot from being razed. He turned it into a warren of restaurants, dance floors, and pub rooms with railroad themes. The place opened to the public in 1988, after long hours of hauling debris and rebuilding the interior of the structure.

Ryan kept the best of the old. The carved graffiti in the woodwork along the trackside windows still carries travelers' mute testimony from the turn of the century. Names, dates, and even short poems are etched into the oak.

◆ **The Depot** (715–682–4200) has become the city's largest tourist attraction, about three or four blocks up from a boardwalk running along the Lake Superior shoreline.

Ryan installed beveled glass, crystal chandeliers, heavy oak stools, autographed paintings of trains, and oodles of other memorabilia. The food in the place is hearty North Woods fare, with moderate to high prices for this region. For instance, Wisconsin sirloin is $12.95, back ribs are $11.99, duck is $15.99. But the ambience is worth a stop. If you prefer simpler fare, excellent burgers are only $4.25. When it first opened, the Depot had a disco in a back room. That area, with its stainless steel dance floor, is now used only for parties and receptions. The place continues to be a great watering hole for the locals, regardless of age.

Anchoring the other end of the boardwalk right on the bay is the new Hotel Chequamegon (715–682–9095), modeled after a landmark hotel that was destroyed by fire in 1955. But the modern hotel could have stepped from the pages of history, opening in 1987 about 100 yards from the original site. The hotel's interior decorating scheme is Victorian with plenty of woodwork, antiques, and ferns. Each of the hotel's suites is named after local communities and decorated with photographs, paintings, and other artifacts donated by residents.

Nice touches include handmade soap in the bathrooms, fresh flowers everywhere, and box lunches that can be prepared for hikers.

The hotel's Fifield Room offers gourmet and regional specialties such as planked whitefish. Its lineup of fresh pasta beats anything this side of the Tiber River. I enjoyed the Superior trout ($12.95) on the one opportunity I had to eat there. A group of us stayed at the hotel for an overnight while snowmobiling in the

**61**

area, taking over part of the dining room. Although the fare was fancy, no one minded our casual attire.

For standard food, and plenty of it, you can't beat the buffet at the Bradley Restaurant across Highway 2 from the Lake Superior shore. I've learned to trust where professional eaters such as truckers and mechanics congregate; the Bradley certainly lives up to that adage. There's plenty of parking around the cozy building, a testimony to accommodating the needs of long-haulers who frequent the restaurant.

Northland College in Ashland is an independent, coed college that focuses on environmental and Native American studies and outdoor education in addition to other liberal arts. It also led the fight to establish Earth Day, a national remembrance of the need to be respectful of the natural world around us. With this empha-sis, the school has an expansive reputation for its conferences and programs on environmental studies. Simply wandering around the campus, perhaps pausing in the ivy-covered Sigurd Olson Environmental Institute, is a respite from the rush of a typical busy day. You'll see more than one canoe mounted atop a car, for students heading out for a field class.

The ◆ **Bad River Chippewa Reservation** at the northern tip of the county annually hosts a powwow the third weekend in August, attracting tribes from around the upper Midwest. The reservation also has a furniture-building school on the reserva-tion, producing everything from picnic tables to desks, and a fac-tory making kits for log homes . . . sort of a giant Lincoln Log set. Both businesses are open to visitors on Tuesday, Thursday, and Friday, located on Highway 2, the major roadway between Ash-land and Bayfield (Bayfield County).

Across the street from the tribal offices are the headquarters of the Great Lakes Fisheries and Game Commission, which moni-tors the Chippewas' hunting and fishing activities guaranteed under treaty rights. Ponds to the rear of the building raise walleyes for stocking lakes around Ashland County.

One of the best places to hear northern Wisconsin's windsong is in the pines of the ◆ **Chequamegon National Forest.** The 848,000 acres of woodlands make up one of the 155 national forests in the United States. Chequamegon (pronounced *Sho-wah-ma-gon*) derives its name from the Chippewa language, "Place of Shallow Water," referring to the nearby placid Chequamegon Bay of rugged Lake Superior. This sprawling forest was replanted in 1933 from overcut and burned land, the result of heavy timber harvesting by private individuals and the government in the 1800s.

Every year, thousands of adventurous types hike, bike, and fish in one of the sections of the forest. The Glidden District is located in Ashland County, and other tracts are in Price and Taylor counties. We took Dan into the Glidden area on his first deep woods camping trip when he was about seven years old, bouncing over the more rugged backtrails via a four-wheel-drive vehicle. My wife, Sandy, and I were working on features for a Rand McNally adventure driving guide at the time. When we got to our Day Lake campsite, we tested our best rod and reel techniques but wound up eating beans and canned stew instead of the walleye that were supposed to go into our skillet that night. But, of course, it must have been the "other guy" who caught the biggie.

So the next day, we packed the poles and hit the backwoods roads crisscrossed by numerous rivers, among them the Moose, Torch, and Chippewa. Dingdong Creek, Hell Hole Creek, Dead Horse Slough, and Rocky Run Rapids may sound like ice cream flavors, but they are the names of smaller streams in the area. Supposedly, there was good fishing, according to the locals. But with our already bruised egos, we decided not to embarrass ourselves anymore, so we headed out of the woods. It was time, however—already late October with the temperature hovering around 20 to 30 degrees.

A good day's jaunt through the Chequamegon, one that includes some fishing and hiking, is along the **North Country Trail.** The tour is a 60-mile link that meanders through the Glidden, Hayward, and Washburn districts of the forest. The route begins on Forest Road 390, about 2 miles west of Mellen, and ends up at County Highway A near Ruth Lake, 5 miles south of Iron River. One of the best stops on the trail is off Forest Road 199 at St. Peter's Dome, a huge outcrop of bald rock from which you can spot Lake Superior about 22 miles to the northeast. It is a steep climb up the back slope of the Dome, fighting your way through the brush. Once on top, you'll find the view worth the struggle. Bring hiking boots if you plan to do much crawling through the underbrush and over the boulders. There is a trail of sorts to the back of the Dome, but it is overhung with thorny berry bushes.

The town of Glidden is the Black Bear Capital of the World, located just outside the forest entrance on Highway 13. The folks here offer a reward to anyone bringing in a bigger bruin (dead, they expect) than the 665-pounder on exhibit in a glass case on the main street overlooking the rest of the city. The bear was nailed in the nearby woods by a hunter who weighed it at the local mill truck scale because no one else, not even the local butcher, had a scale big enough to do justice to the brute.

Here's a hint for keeping those walking floor rugs out of your camp at night. If you don't take precautions, you could have a real problem on your hands. *Keep all food hanging high in trees or inside locked car trunks. Be sure everything is out of reach of scratching claws.* Chequamegon's bears have been known to demolish coolers and food lockers in their foraging. And they are not playful teddies on a picnic.

## BARRON COUNTY

The ◆**Rutabaga Festival** in Cumberland elevates this lowly veggie to heights it probably never realized it could attain. Held the fourth weekend in August, the festival features a 130-unit parade, the Rutabaga Walk & Run, an art and craft show, a hot pepper–eating contest, a Rutabaga Queen contest, and the Rutabaga Olympics. In the latter, rutabagas are tossed, turned, and tumbled in a variety of family-themed events guaranteed for a laugh and a lot of fun. Cumberland is easy to find, located as it is on State Highway 48, west of Rice Lake. The city chose the rutabaga as its prime image maker because of the numbers of farmers in the area who grow the crop. But when not munching rutabagas, you can hike the Ice Age, Tuscobia, Old Indian, and Old Swamp trails that cut through or near the city. The well-marked pathways make Barron County an outdoor lover's paradise.

Hikers also love the Blue Hills of eastern Barron County, noted for their rugged, smoky appearance. The scenery is especially delightful in spring and autumn when the fog hangs heavily around the valleys and deep gullies that score the region. Some of the ridges there are as high as 20,000 feet. While the area's rough edges were smoothed down by glacial action eons ago, there are still plenty of opportunities for a leg-stretching meander.

# BAYFIELD COUNTY

Bayfield County is the largest of all the Wisconsin counties, yet it doesn't have a stoplight. Honest.

Almost 10 percent of the fresh water in the world is around the Apostle Islands, according to environmentalists. The sprinkling of islands dotting Lake Superior off the coast of Bayfield County were left there by the glaciers.

The ice drifts left behind huge mounds of rubble on their retreat northward eons ago. An early missionary who couldn't quite add gave the archipelago its name. Actually there are twenty-two islands, ranging in size from the 3-acre Gull Island to the 22 square miles of Madeline Island. Long Island is only 10 feet above the waterline. The entire area is federally protected, as part of the Apostle Islands National Lakeshore.

Camping is possible on seventeen of the islands. Interpretive programs include lighthouse tours on Raspberry Island, campfire programs at night on South Twin, Rocky, and Stockton islands, and a tour of a commercial fishing camp on Manitou Island. For cruises around the islands, if you don't own your own sailboat, take the ◆**Apostle Islands Cruise Service** tours (715–779–3925), which operate out of Bayfield. The line offers various excursions, including sunset voyages and a Sunday brunch voyage.

In the winter of 1988, I snowmobiled across the frozen 2.6-mile lake strait to Madeline Island in the predawn hours. It was a time when even the late stars seemed frozen against the sky. The ice bridge linking the island to the mainland is a travel-at-your-own-risk proposition, but generally quite safe in the minus 20 degrees of a January predawn. Cars and trucks even take the route regularly in the winter. When the thaw comes and the summer finally arrives, the **Madeline Island Ferry Line** (715–747–2051) beats swimming.

The island has a nifty museum located one block from the ferry dock. The facility is operated by the Wisconsin Historical Society and is packed with artifacts dating from the earliest Native Americans to the white settlers. An Indian burial ground is one-half mile from the dock as you drive around the marina. Several of the tombstones date back 200 years. For details about the island, contact the Madeline Island Chamber of Commerce, Box 274, La Point 54850 (715–474–2801).

**65**

Another visitor information center is run by the National Park Service, located in the old **Bayfield Courthouse,** 415 Washington Avenue. The building is open seven days a week from May through October and six days a week from November through April. For specific information on the islands, including the interpretive programs, contact the Apostle Islands National Lakeshore, Route 1, Box 4, Bayfield 54814 (715–779–3397).

The area is dotted with wrecks, remains of vessels caught in the headwinds that howl around Bayfield County, a thumb that juts into Lake Superior's belly. One way to explore some of the underwater artifacts is scuba diving. Ship and Dive Charters can provide equipment, guides, and other diving services for adventurers wishing to take a plunge. Contact them at First Street and Manypenny Avenue, Bayfield 54814 (715–779–5000). The waters around the island are very tricky, with crosscurrents and eddies that can spell trouble to any inexperienced divers. It is wise to check with the pros before attempting any deep water investigation.

Bayfield is a pleasant resort community, with the usual collection of antique shops, small restaurants, and motels/hotels. One of the best rainbows we ever saw arched over the marina there after a brief summer storm a few years ago.

The little park at the corner of Rittenhouse Avenue and Front Street was freshly washed by the rain. The sailboats were bobbing quietly in the smooth water; only the clinking and tinkling of chains on metal masts could be heard. The sun was dipping low behind us, with just enough light to pop that brilliant rainbow out from the dark clouds scudding over the eastern background.

The **Old Rittenhouse Inn** (715–779–5111) is a restored Victorian mansion dating from the 1890s, now a bed and breakfast with rates ranging from $79 to $179 per night. The dining room is open to the public, offering the most elegant meals in the north country. Try the homemade lemon cheesecake with glazed raspberries, made by Mary Phillips, who owns the Rittenhouse with her husband, Jerry. The Rittenhouse hosts special programs throughout the year, ranging from concerts to Christmas displays.

The **C-Side Inn** is about 6 miles west of Washburn on Highway C, along the eastern edge of Bayfield County's northern hunk of the Chequamegon. It's a perfect stop for snowmobilers and skiers. A huge pot of homemade chicken soup is always bubbling in the kitchen, to go along with the homemade bread served with slabs of peanut butter and strawberry jam. The food is stick-to-your-ribs fare, just the thing needed when rumbling through the forest's snowbound **Valhalla Recreation Area.** If you prefer fancier fare, have steak, eggs, toast, and hashbrowns.

**Nepp's Bar** on Highway G, 7 miles west of Ashland (Ashland County), is another good layover. Run by Millie Augustine, the place is packed with stuffed animals, including a cigar-smoking coyote. Actually, the coyote doesn't puff the stogie tucked rakishly into one side of its grinning mouth, but it looks ready to at any minute. Millie took over the place when her husband died a few years ago. She's always glad to tell how they moved the original bar up from the nearby bottomlands where it had regularly been flooded out each spring. Today, the building is on higher and drier land.

The ◆**Big Top Chautauqua** in Washburn brings alive the spirit and fun of the old-time traveling tent shows of the nineteenth century. Performances are held from early July through Labor Day in a breezy park overlooking Lake Superior. For a schedule, contact Warren Nelson, Box 455, Washburn 54891 (715–742–3902 or 715–373–5851).

## CHIPPEWA COUNTY

The **Gateway Inn** hugs a corner of Highways 64 and 40, 3 miles northeast of Bloomer. The Gateway is one of several north country locales that has had a checkered past. It allegedly was a favorite layover for Chicago gangster Al Capone, who often vacationed in Wisconsin. He'd stop to visit friends, have a sandwich, and then move on. According to current owner Rick Mitchell, illegal booze was made in a backyard still and stored in a thirty-gallon copper tank. The receptacle was hidden under the Gateway's phone booth.

Mitchell claims a gangster's ghost named Frankie haunts his place in a friendly fashion. You probably won't see him, especially floating around dinnertime, which runs from 5:00 to 10:00 P.M. weekdays and 5:00 to 11:00 P.M. weekends, with lunches from 11:00 A.M. to 2:00 P.M. daily through the summer. It's time then to concentrate on the veal or prime rib, rather than seek out specters. Call (715) 568–2465 for reservations on the weekends.

## CLARK COUNTY

One of the most poignant retreats in Wisconsin is the ◆ **High-Ground Veterans Memorial Park,** about 12 miles west of Neillsville on Highway 51. Overlooking a deep valley, High-Ground was dedicated in 1988 as the state's official memorial to its Vietnam vets. It's a powerful place, where emotional reunions constantly occur among men and women who survived that ugly conflict.

A statue there features several wounded soldiers and a nurse. Under the nurse's cape hang 1,215 dog tags, each with the name of a Wisconsinite who died during the war. The wind causes the tags to tinkle gently, a sound that no one forgets.

Regular ceremonies are held at the park, which is constantly being expanded. Memorials to World War II and Korean veterans are also being planned for the site.

## DOUGLAS COUNTY

The city of Superior is the largest community in northern Wisconsin. Founded as a mining center, it is now a commercial hub for the North Woods counties. Hugging the south rim of Lake Superior, it is linked to Duluth, Minnesota, by the Richard I. Bong Memorial Bridge. The gracefully curving structure is named after the World War II flying ace born in nearby Poplar, a fifteen-minute drive east of town. In the late 1980s, Superior was used as a setting for a film starring Jessica Lange. The location scouts came to town several times seeking picturesque sites draped with birch trees. The advance crews fell in love with the entire community and convinced the director to expand his shooting operation around the vicinity.

The ◆ **SS** *Meteor,* the world's last remaining whaleback freighter, is anchored at the Superior docks off Barker's Island. You can climb its decks and investigate the pilothouse and gallery. The old ore vessel gets its name from the odd-appearing whale shape that provided extra stability in rolling waters. The ship was launched in 1896. The museum (715–394–7716) is open from 10:00 A.M. to 5:00 P.M. Memorial Day through Labor Day. There are extended hours until 7:00 P.M. in July. It is open weekends in September and October. From July 3 through August 11, guides are on duty from 10:00 A.M. to 5:00 P.M.

For more maritime history, the **Fairlawn Mansion and Museum** has an extensive display of photographs and artifacts on Superior's shipping industry. The restored forty-two-room mansion is open year-round from 9:00 A.M. to 5:00 P.M. daily. The museum is located at 906 E. Second Street (715–394–5712). Tickets for both Fairlawn and the SS *Meteor* are $4.00 for adults, $3.00 for students thirteen to eighteen and seniors sixty and above, and $2.00 for youngsters six to twelve.

There's always a hot time in Superior, at least during the summer, when the old **Firehouse and Police Museum** is open (10:00 A.M. to 5:00 P.M.). The red brick building can't be missed at the junction of 23rd Avenue East and Fourth Street (Highways 2 and 53). Admission is $2.75 for adults and $2.25 for kids twelve and under. Among the artifacts on display is a 1906 steam pumper.

Douglas County's ◆**Amnicon Falls State Park** is one of the state's most photogenic waterfalls, crying for a calendar cover shot. The 800-acre park is located on Highway 2, about 10 miles east of Superior. The Amnicon River divides around an island in the center of the park, with a covered bridge linking the banks. Good photo vantage points are from the bridge or from either shore.

One of the best trout flowages in the county is the Brule River, which passes through Douglas County from Solon Springs into Lake Superior. Presidents Grant and Cleveland enjoyed fly casting on the river, and Silent Cal Coolidge had his summer White House at a resort there for several years. Cal never talked much about his secret fishing holes, but local bait shop owners will tell you everything you need to know about the entire stretch of river. Part of the waterway meanders through the rugged Brule River Forest.

## FOREST COUNTY

"Larry the Logroller" is Wabeno's famous attraction. The statue of a timbercutter stands 21 feet 9 inches tall, symbolizing the area's main industry as well as providing a mascot for the town's high school sports teams. The statue is next to the Wabeno High School band shell in town. Straight-backed Larry looks a little stiff, as if he was chopping wood too long, but he's a good backdrop for a family portrait.

Laona is in the heart of the ◈ **Nicolet National Forest,** where many of the local loggers still work—cutting out about 200,000 cords of hardwood per year. The wood is sent to mills in the Fox River Valley to the south. The Nicolet Forest encompasses about 651,000 acres, within which are the headwaters for the Wolf, Pine, Popple, Oconto, and Peshtigo rivers. The Nicolet was named after Jean Nicolet, the French explorer who "discovered" Wisconsin in 1634.

While in the Nicolet forest, look for the MacArthur Pine, named for the famed general. The tree is one of the oldest in the nation, standing 148 feet high and having a circumference of 17 feet. The tree was old when Nicolet and his voyageurs were first finding their way to the southlands some three hundred years ago. To find the tree, turn north onto State Highway 139 just as you leave the village of Cavour to the west. (Cavour is 8 miles north of Laona on Highway 8.) Continue to Forest Road 2166 near Newald and turn west to Forest Road 2167. Make a sharp turn north and you'll spot the pine towering above its neighbors.

Laona has been putting on a Community Soup annually for the past sixty-plus years the first Sunday of every August. Townsfolk donate the ingredients for the homemade vegetable soup that is made in large cast-iron pots over an open fire. The only requirement for eating is that you bring your own bowl and spoon. Some of the fun is coming to the city park to watch the preparations, which begin about 6:00 A.M. The soup is simmered until noon, when serving starts. The recipe includes some secret ingredients, but generally it contains fresh onions, carrots, celery, potatoes, beans, and whatever else might be around a garden.

The soup-serving tradition started years ago when neighbors got together for a friendly outing. The confab grew so large that the Laona Lions Club took over operations a few years ago to help coordinate the event.

Laona is also home to the **Camp Five Lumberjack Train,** a steam train that operates Monday through Saturday from June to late August. Camp Five is a typical turn-of-the-century lumber camp, with an environmental hike nearby and a country store on the grounds at the junction of Highways 8 and 32

(715–674–3414, summer; 715–845–5544, winter). The train ride through the woods is fun, giving kids the chance to see a working locomotive up close.

Forest County has another interesting Rustic Road that extends through the woodlands for 7.4 miles off Highway 70. It meanders across Brule Creek along Fishel Road to Cary Dam Road to Lake View Drive, concluding in the hamlet of Alvin on Highway 55. The village is about 2 miles south of the Michigan border.

On the first weekend in August, the northland's best bluegrass bands gather at the Mole Lake Indian Reservation for a four-day round of music and hand-clapping good times. The village is 8 miles south of Crandon. For a schedule of performers, call 715–478–2604 or write the ◆ **Great Northern Bluegrass Festival,** Crandon 54520. Many nationally known entertainers drop by for some pick-up singing.

## IRON COUNTY

The **Frontier Bar** on Highway 2 near Saxon is a loud, happy place. It's the jumping-off point on the Iron Horse Snowmobile Trail for a 20-mile run northward through the Bad River Indian Reservation in next-door Ashland County. Tucked off the highway, about 7 miles south of Lake Superior, the Frontier is the place to hang out, tell a few lies, and eat chili—not necessarily in that order. Owned by John and Kay Innes, longtime North Woods residents from nearby Cedar, the Frontier outdoes fast-food joints with its hefty burgers. If you are the last of the big spenders, add some cheese for only a dime. In the wintertime, Innes serves up a "snowshoe," a schnapps with a brandy.

Mercer is proud of its title, "the Loon Capital." The large birds have a distinctive, haunting call that echoes over the lakes and forests of Wisconsin. They are such a part of the North Woods world that Mercer dedicated a large statue to the fowl on Highway 51 at the southern outskirts of town. The 16-foot-high bird is in a little park adjacent to the town's information center. The big bird weighs 2,000 pounds and contains a speaker with a tape recording explaining all the loon calls and facts about the bird's habitat. There is a serious reason for the Mercer display as well. It is a reminder that the lakes in Iron County provide one of the few prime breeding grounds for the large waterbird.

## LANGLADE COUNTY

The roar of white water is music to the ears of outdoors fans in Langlade, Marinette, Menominee, and Oconto counties where caneoing, kayaking, or rafting are more than just Huck Finn adventures. Using rubber rafts, the rides can be slow, easy drifting or furious careening along the Wolf, Peshtigo, or Menominee rivers. The routes twist and turn through the pine woods, with action paced by the height of the water during each season. Commercial raft operators usually hit the water from Memorial Day through Labor Day on the Menominee and from mid-April to late October on the Peshtigo and Wolf. The Menominee is dam controlled, which determines the amount of high water, so it's always good to call an outfitter before arrival to check on water levels.

Gear is simple. Use tennis shoes or rubber-soled shoes because rafts have soft bottoms that can get slippery when racing the rapids. Often, regular riders use wet suits when the weather turns chilly. Windbreakers are important in early spring. There's no sense in being uncomfortable. Rafts hold from two to four persons, with trips ranging from one to five hours.

Newcomers to the rafting scene will enjoy a mild ride on Langlade County's Wolf River, which alternates between rugged boulders with gentle waves to bedrock that churns the water into a hearty froth. There are plenty of fast chutes for stomach-tingling action.

The higher stretch of the river between Hollister and Langlade offers long stretches of smooth water. In the lower section of the Wolf, the water picks up speed through Boy Scout Rapids. This is not a place for beginners, edging as it does into a rocky funnel that is strewn with boulders. A narrow channel follows, where rocks are close enough to shave a preteen. The run then slides back onto smooth water.

Quality outfitters include Jesse's ◆ **Wolf River Lodge** on Highway 55 north of Langlade (715–882–2182) and Shotgun Eddy's Rafting on Highway 55 just south of Langlade in Menominee County (715–882–4461 or 414–494–3782).

## LINCOLN COUNTY

For good reason, ◆ **Merrill** is called the "City of Parks." The town has nine major parks within its boundaries, making it the

picnic capital of the north country. Green grass, brilliant flowers, huge shade trees, playgrounds, and shelters seem to pop up
from every corner. For an excursion outside of town, **Council
Grounds State Park** is located on State Highway 107 only a
few miles northwest of Merrill. Traditionally a gathering spot
for Chippewa Indians, the area became the hub of the North
Woods logging industry. Between the 1870s and early 1900s,
hundreds of lumberjacks chopped and sawed the towering pine
that once ruled the forestlands. Some 600 million board-feet of
timber were eventually floated downstream on the Wisconsin
River from Merrill's immediate vicinity during the boom days.
Council Grounds Park now is much quieter and trees have been
replanted, so now you could barely tell that this landscape once
had the appearance of a crew cut. The park has some excellent
swimming areas (keep an eye on the kids because there are no
lifeguards), plus boating and cross-country skiing in season.
There is also a breathtaking (literally) exercise trail that weaves
in and out of the trees, so get in shape.

## MARINETTE COUNTY

Few people outside Wisconsin known much about Peshtigo. In
1871, however, a raging forest fire destroyed much of Marinette
County's drought-stricken timber, taking the town with it on
October 8. The fire swept through the community on the same
day as the Great Chicago Fire, which pushed the incident onto
the back pages of the nation's newspapers. Yet the Wisconsin
incident was more horrifying. Between 600 and 800 persons
died in the Wisconsin fire, more than five times the number
who perished in Chicago.

The Peshtigo River meanders past the Badger Paper Mill, one of
the mainstays of the town's economy. The river itself saved hundreds of persons, who survived the nineteenth-century fire by
leaping into the steaming water. The inferno is remembered in the
❖**Peshtigo Fire Museum,** which is highlighted by a huge
painting depicting that fateful day and the role of the river as a
lifesaver. The museum is in an old church that replaced one burned
in the forest fire. Its display cases are carefully filled with melted
coins, broken dishes, and other artifacts donated by area residents.
A mound near the museum is a common grave for 350 unidentified

victims of the fire. The museum is one block north of Highway 41 on Oconto Avenue. Turn at Ellis Street, and you'll see the building.

The town is laid out much as it was before the fire: along the east and west sides of the river. Streets are wide and lined with maples and oaks. Gone are the huge pines that ranged all the way from Green Bay toward the Michigan border.

Things are generally quiet now on the Peshtigo, but there's a 5-mile stretch of water called Roaring Rapids that puts a rafter's heart in his or her mouth. The river rolls through the thick forest, cutting like a knife through hot cheese into Five-Foot Falls, which has a vertical drop of bedrock and only one way to go—straight ahead with a yell and all the pumping adrenaline you can muster.

The chute whaps rafts into a sheet of smooth water near the left bank, but rowers have to watch out for upcoming boulders. Horse Race Rapids is the longest ride on the river, where the narrow chute cuts through steep cliffs. High waves are kicked up over the rocks, and it takes lots of extra muscle and steering expertise to battle through without being swamped. That 30 or so yards of heart-murmur slides into several tight corners and drops over submerged rocks into a quiet pool where you can get your head back on straight again, according to experienced rafters.

The Menominee River, which forms the border between the state of Michigan and Marinette County, is a good rafting locale, according to friends who take the white-water route quite often. They suggest putting in at **Little Quinness Falls Dam,** for a 2-mile run through heavy woods and into a short stretch of rapids. The first drop, according to ace rafter John Shepard, is about 7 feet on a "pour-over" called Mishicot Falls. There's a tricky backwash at the base of the waterfall, he warns.

The county is noted for its waterfalls, the bane of the lumberjacks but a boon to photographers. The loggers hated coming to the narrow rapids that could often cause jams, lost time, and deaths. Nobody enjoyed ramming the timber over the waterfalls. Today's visitor doesn't have to be concerned about those problems. Finding the best picture angle is enough.

The county's most picturesque falls are just off the meandering Parkway Road in the western stretch of the county. Some of the roughest falls in this area have been channeled or partially tamed over the past generations by artificial dams. To get to ❖ **High Falls Dam,** take High Falls Road off Parkway Road. The dam creates the 1,700-acre High Falls Flowage. Just to the north of the dam a mile or so is **Twin Bridge Park,** which provides another good spot to see the High Falls Flowage. The park is also off Parkway Road. You need to be careful at Veteran's Falls (just off Parkway Road in **Veterans' Memorial Park** on the Thunder River) because of the steep slopes dropping down to the falls themselves. Be sure to wear hiking boots or other strong shoes. A picturesque little wooden bridge angling high over the rapids is a perfect setting for autumn camping and picnicking.

To see the Caldron Falls Dam, take Boat Landing 8 Road off Parkway. The dam creates the 1,200-acre **Caldron Falls Flowage,** where a boat launch is available. McClintock Falls is located in **McClintock Park** off Parkway Road. The falls is actually a series of rapids and white water with several bridges leapfrogging from bank to bank. This is one of the nicest picnic areas in Marinette County. Strong Falls is in **Goodman Park** on the Peshtigo River, off Parkway Road. Many hiking trails wander through the dense forest and brushland in the park itself. The park planners provided log shelters in the area, handy refuges in case of rain.

Other waterfalls in the county are also easily reached off the beaten path. To see ◈ **Twelve Foot Falls,** scene of several television commercials, take Lily Lake Road south off Highway 8 to Twelve Foot Falls Road. Several magnificent drops make up the waterway. Each has its own name: Horseshoe Falls, Eighteen Foot Falls, Eight Foot Falls, and Bull Falls. We like Horseshoe best because of the surrounding framework of trees.

The list continues, a fact making waterfall lovers gleeful. For Long Slide Falls, drive along Morgan Park Road to the east off Highway 141. A small sign marks the direction, so be alert, or you might miss the turnoff. Park your car and take the short walking trail to the falls themselves. A county park with camping, swimming, and picnicking is up the road to the east. Piers Gorge is a white-water rapids area along the Menominee River in the far northern section of the county. To get to the viewing area, take Highway 8 when it branches to the east off Highway 141 just before you get to the Michigan-Wisconsin border. On the northeast side of the county's border with Michigan is Pemenee Falls, which is a really wild stretch of the Menominee. You'll find the spot just to the left as you enter Michigan on County Highway Z.

◈ **Dave's Falls** is my personal favorite, located south of

**75**

Amberg on the Pike River. There's a county park there with a neat wooden bridge arching high over the water. A nineteenth-century folk song tells the sad lament of how a logger named Dave died while breaking up a jam on the river in that location. Ever since that accident, the falls has carried his name.

The ◆**American Outdoor Learning Center** near Crivitz knows how to accommodate folks wanting to learn to white-water raft, canoe, or backpack. The center offers lessons and classes in many outdoor disciplines, with an emphasis on safety and skill. For information, contact the center at Box 133, Athelstane 54104 (715–757–3811).

With all this water in Marinette County, remember that one-third of all the best trout streams in the state are located here.

## Menominee County

One of the country's largest and most complete logging museums is located on Highway 47 and County VV, on the Wolf River at Grignon Rapids in Keshena. Unless you knew it was there, however, you might miss the facility. The camp (715–799–3757) is on the 230,000 acres of the ◆**Menominee Indian Reservation** about 168 miles north of Milwaukee. Indian guides take visitors through the seven log buildings that have been rebuilt in the heavy forest. A cook shack is complete with table settings and a well-stocked kitchen. The blacksmith shop, woodworker's building, and bunkhouse are outfitted as well with the appropriate nineteenth-century details. The camp is open from 9:00 A.M. to 4:00 P.M. daily except Monday during the summer and on September and October weekends. Admission is $2.00 for adults and 50 cents for children under sixteen.

The museum is one of several economic development packages in Menominee County aimed at making the tribe more self-sufficient. Other industries include a sawmill, bingo parlor, and a rafting outfitter to guide travelers on the 59-mile stretch of the Wolf River that meanders through tribal lands.

## Oconto County

Southwest from Peshtigo is Oconto, on the sun-dappled shore of Green Bay. Camping for recreational vehicles is available at the

**North Shore Recreation Area** on the edge of the bay, just a few minutes' walk to the banks. You can fish from land or use waders to get a few steps closer to the chinook and trout that range in the murky waters offshore.

As with Peshtigo, Oconto's neighbor just to the north, a forest fire almost destroyed the town in 1871. A rain came just at the right time, as the flames were creeping to within a few blocks of some of the stately mansions that still can be seen along Park Avenue and its side streets. Edward Scofield, Wisconsin's governor from 1897 to 1901, lived in Oconto for a time. His home at 610 Main Street was built in 1868, next door to the Bond house, whose occupants ran a pickle factory. These magnificent old houses were among the dozens saved by that lucky downpour.

About two miles west of Oconto is ◆**Copper Culture Mound State Park,** where artifacts have been found from a clan of prehistoric people. The Copper Culture Museum (414–834–2260) displays many of these items in a building adjacent to the park. Apparently, these ancient craftworkers mined the copper from nearby deposits, made tools and other items from the precious metal, and traded with groups as far away as the Gulf of Mexico. The museum is open from June through Labor Day. Donations are accepted.

## ONEIDA COUNTY

The hungry hodag lurks in the woods around Rhinelander, a town where tall tales maybe could be true. At least the only place in the world where you'll see a hodag is in the logging museum in the city's Pioneer Park. The mythical monster was dreamed up in 1896 by some of the loggers who worked in the forests. They supposedly captured a 7-foot-long hairy beast with huge horns and teeth, keeping it "alive" in a pit behind the house of one of the practical jokers. Nobody was too upset to discover that the men had assembled the beast with ox hides and claws made from bent steel rods. The hodag had captured the town's interest and became a local legend.

The ◆**Rhinelander Logging Museum** is at the junction of Highways 8 and 47 (715–369–5004). In addition to the hodag, the museum shows off equipment used by frontier woodcutters.

The museum is open from 1:00 to 6:30 P.M. daily from about May 20 until mid-September. Donations are accepted.

Adjacent to the logging facility is the **Civilian Conservation Corps Museum,** which should bring back memories to anyone who served in the CCC during the Depression. The replica of a typical camp located in a one-room schoolhouse was opened in 1983 for the fiftieth anniversary of the government-sponsored conservation work brigade. More than 3 million persons worked in the corps between 1933 and 1942, preserving and maintaining forests and waterways. Former CCC volunteers staff the museum from Memorial Day through Labor Day, telling about their work in the woods. Photos, uniforms, and tools from the era are displayed in the barracks and other buildings. Donations are accepted.

On the last Saturday in September, the folks in Minocqua celebrate Beef-O-Rama, where anyone who wants to fix a giant pot roast (provided by the local Chamber of Commerce) can compete for prizes. Celebrity judges get to sample upwards of sixty roasts before choosing a winner. Prior to announcing the victors, the chefs parade down the main street to a local park where the meat is made into sandwiches.

I took daughter Kate and one of her friends, plus son Steve, there for a recent party. We couldn't look at another roast beef for months.

Minocqua and Milwaukee, incidentally, have launched into a Sister City tourism promotion to encourage a rural-urban getaway experience.

## POLK COUNTY

On the outskirts of St. Croix Falls along Highway 8 is the ◆ **Ice Age Interpretive Center** at Interstate Park. Some splendid geological formations in the park's canyonlands are sure to get camera shutters clicking. A highly instructive film on the impact of the glaciers throughout the region should capture the attention of even the most wiggly tyke. The center is open from 9:00 A.M. to 5:00 P.M. Memorial Day through Labor Day and from noon to 4:00 P.M. daily the rest of the year. You'll need a state park sticker for admission, which can be secured at the center (715–483–3747).

But if the film still doesn't keep the kids' attention, drive 3 miles west on Highway 8 to **Fawn Doe Rosa Park,** where they can feed and pet deer and other animals. The park is open from 9:30 A.M. to 8:00 P.M. mid-May through September. Call (715) 483–3747 if you need more information.

## Price County

◆ **Timm's Hill,** the highest point in Wisconsin, is 6 miles east of Omega, just before you get to the crossroads village of Spirit. Timm's Hill is 1,951 feet (594.8 meters) above sea level. An observation tower rears over the treetops for an even more expansive view of the countryside. On a blustery autumn day, middle son Steve and I climbed up there as the wind tugged our coattails. A hint: Don't look down. But once on the top, the sight was spectacular . . . even if it was a white-knuckler.

◆ **Wisconsin Concrete Park** on Highway 13 South in Phillips is definitely a difficult—or should I say hard—place to miss. Some 200 statues made from concrete portray cowboys on horseback, deer, bear, Native Americans, and a plethora of other items from the imagination of the late Fred Smith. When Smith retired from logging, he took up sculpture and today is considered one of America's foremost folk artists. For a special effect, Smith put bits of broken glass into his dozens of whimsical forms, all of which seem to smile back at the observer. The park is open year-round; admission is free. For information call (715) 339–4505.

## St. Croix County

Hudson looks much like the Hudson River Valley of New York State. At least that's what the original settlers in the area thought, so they figured the name would fit their community as well. The ◆ **Octagon House** is the local history center, at 1004 Third Street (715–386–2654), on the north end of the town's business district off Highway 35. There's a magnificent old grand piano in the old home's living room. Looking at it, one would never guess that it was twice dumped into the Mississippi River on its delivery run here in the mid-1800s. The Octagon House is open 10:00 A.M. to noon and 2:00 to 4:30 P.M., Tuesday through Saturday; and 2:00 to 4:30 P.M. on Sunday, May through October and December 1 to 15. It is closed Monday. Admission is charged.

**79**

Near the city, a puffing, rumbling, rocking, and rolling engine swings quickly around the track. A full head of steam greets the passengers waiting for a ride on the **St. Croix Railroad.** Everyone piles on, a bit cramped maybe, but ready to roll. With Bob Ahrens at the throttle, you know you'll keep to the schedule. It's not a hard run, with only a 4-foot-high engine and several 6-foot-long passenger cars traveling more than 7,000 feet of track. But that's the fun of it. The "toy line" railroad is Ahrens's plaything, a train set to end all train sets, with an engine that burns crushed charcoal. In fact, the entrance to this place has a sign that reads CAUTION MAN AT PLAY. He laid the aluminum rails himself, spacing them through his eight acres of valleyland. Call (715) 386–1871 or 386–3311 for the April through October seasonal hours for the St. Croix Railroad. There is a charge for tickets.

The ❖**Apple River** in Somerset is the best place in the state to try your hand, or bottom, at tubing. Numerous outfitters throughout the area rent inner tubes for swift rides along the flowage. The water isn't usually deep, but be sure to wear tennis shoes because of the rocky river bottom. Even kids can enjoy the ride, swirling as they do through the eddies and across quiet pools. The rental companies will pick you up at the end of the hour or half-day run. Watch out for sunburn, however. The glare from the stream can bake fair skin quicker than a microwave.

One good outfitter in the area, a member of the Hudson Area Chamber of Commerce (800–657–6775), is the Apple River Campground (800–637–8936 or 715–247–3378). Rates for tubing are $6.50 for adults and $5.50 for juniors. You need to add an extra dollar for Saturday and Sunday. Runs are offered during daylight hours Monday through Friday and on weekends May through April.

## SAWYER COUNTY

There was a time when the North Woods attracted another tourist element, one that was not really welcomed. Chicago mobsters often came to the quiet lakes and woods to escape the literal and figurative heat of the Windy City. They brought their nervousness with them, however. ❖**The Hideout** is one of the most extensive retreats used by mobster Al Capone, who favored fishing almost as much as rum running. Fieldstone pillars guard the entrances to a 400-acre estate near Couderay that he used to rest and recuperate. The architecture inside the grounds includes a gun tower, bunkhouse, cell, and other buildings utilized by gang members when they vacationed in Sawyer County. An eight-car garage on the property has been converted into a restaurant and bar. Don't be surprised to see a mannequin of the notorious gangster in the main lodge, seated at a table in the dining room.

The Hideout (715–945–2746) is open for tours daily from noon until early evening the weekend before Memorial Day through mid-September. Late in the autumn until the third weekend of October, the site is open only Friday, Saturday, and Sunday. Tours cost $5.50 for adults and $2.75 for children six to eleven. The place is still secluded, set in the woods 17 miles southeast of Hayward. To get there, take County Trunk B east to NN, south on NN to N, east on N for two blocks to CC, then east on CC one-half mile to the entrance.

The world's largest muskie rears over the trees in Hayward, marking the site of the ◆ **National Fresh Water Fishing Hall of Fame.** The five-story glass-fiber structure houses a large portion of the museum, with its dated outboard engines, lures, and stuffed fish. The lower jaw of the giant muskie is a platform

**National Fresh Water Fishing Hall of Fame**

on which several weddings have been held. Even if you aren't die-hard fisherfolks, wandering among the exhibits makes a good layover for anyone on a rainy weekday afternoon when vacation time is running short. Admission is $4.00 for adults, $2.50 for kids under eighteen, and $1.50 for youngsters ten and under. The museum is open daily from 9:30 A.M. to 5:00 P.M., April 15 to November 1. Only the offices are open in winter. The museum is located on the south side of Hayward at the corner of County Trunk B and Highway 27 (715–634–4440).

Hayward is also site of the ◆**Lumberjack World Championships** held each July, with contestants from Australia, New Zealand, and the United States. They compete in ax chopping, tree climbing, bucksawing, and other robust events. This is a chance for you to wear red flannel shirts, overalls, and wide suspenders. Everyone else in town does that. For information contact the Hayward Area Association of Commerce, 101 W. First Street, Box 726, Hayward 54843–0726; (800) 826–3474 or (715) 634–8662.

## TREMPEALEAU COUNTY

Trempealeau County's western boundary is the turgid, mud-black Mississippi River. Catfish roll to the surface, and muskrats splash in the backwater sloughs. The waterway, fed by the fast-flowing Black River, anchors the bottom of the county and gives life to its surroundings.

We love watching fat barges swinging downstream, loaded with grain, lumber, or petroleum products from the Twin Cities, heading to the far Southland and the Gulf of Mexico. The barges, shepherded by a rumbling tugboat, are aimed carefully for the entrance to ◆**Lock and Dam No. 6** at Trempealeau, one of the major links on the upper river's navigational channels.

An overlook near a parking lot alongside the dam provides a great vantage point for watching the river traffic during the spring to autumn shipping season. You can almost stand on top of the barges as they are pushed through the locks. Then, all of a sudden, the barges drop down to the lower level and continue on their journey to New Orleans. In addition to the bigger vessels, more than 6,000 pleasure craft use the locks each year. Lines of little fishing boats, sleek canoes, and jaunty cabin cruisers hug the lock walls like a convoy of ducklings before they are also dropped or raised to the next level. The complex consists of a main lock and an auxiliary structure recently completed by the Army Corps of Engineers, plus a concrete dam and an earthen dike extending across the wet bottomlands. The foot of the spillway near the Minnesota side provides good fishing.

While in town, stay at the comfortably funky old **Trempealeau Hotel** (608–534–6898). Owner Bill King takes very good care of his guests. Rooms range from $27 to $32.

North of Trempealeau is Galesville, at the junction of Highway 35/54 and 53. The town's **Mill Road Café** is just across Beaver Creek from High Cliff Park and its bluffside hiking trail.

The Café is a self-serve restaurant that has some delightfully off-the-beaten-path eats, drinks, and music. New Ulm's Ulmer Lager beer and build-your-own turkey sandwiches with sprouts and tomatoes go down well when listening to High and Outside or another bluegrass/folk music group.

Jane Herbert has owned the Mill Road Café since moving to Wisconsin from California in the mid-1980s. While on earlier antique foraging trips, she came across Galesville and fell in love with the Mill, once a pottery and health food deli. Jane's interest in antiquing is still alive. The Mill Road is comfortably cluttered with farm auction and garage sale treasures. For dessert fans, she makes a bran muffin that seems to weigh in at a delicious ton or three. Really, it's not that heavy, but it's excellent enough to bag some for home.

## VILAS COUNTY

Don Baertschy is Vilas County's best promoter. He runs ◆**Baertschy's Colonial House** restaurant in Eagle River and is not bashful about extolling the wonders of the North Woods and his county. Baertschy has been serving ice cream from behind the counter of his Colonial House for more than a decade, accommodating the local and tourist trade in this popular fishing/hunting community. After managing some of the state's best restaurants, he and his wife, Violet, decided to move to Eagle River and open a place of their own. Since his family used to own a dairy in southern Wisconsin, he knows his milk products and puts out only a top-grade ice cream that's about 15 percent butterfat, almost double some commercial brands.

Solid old oak booths line the walls. Real marble tops the tables. A tin ceiling provides the final old-fashioned look. Prices are low to moderate, including those for Baertschy's homemade pizza. I swear on a stack of muskies that it is probably the best pizza north of Highway 21, that figurative Tension Line that emotionally divides the laid-back vacation land of northern Wisconsin from the frenzied hustle and bustle of southern Wisconsin.

The Colonial House is open daily from 8:00 A.M. until 11:00 P.M. in the summer and from 8:00 A.M. to 6:00 P.M. in the winter. The restaurant is closed only on Mother's and Father's days, Thanksgiving, and Christmas.

The **Bear Bar** (715–686–2280) in Winchester is Art LaHa's trophy room. Life-size moose and caribou, oodles of ducks, muskrats, mink, and other critters peek out from every cranny in the joint. You can't miss the Bear Bar. It's under the third street light in town. The Chicago Pub and D & D's Pizza are under the second. Coming in on County W from Highway 51, that's about all that's in Winchester. Nearby lakes have picturesque names: No Man's, Papoose, Spider, North and South Turtle.

LaHa is a born and bred hunter who has roamed the world stalking trophies. He used to travel the country with his film, *No Land for the Timid,* which depicted him going after polar bears, whales, and other big game. The film is now a video that plays continuously in the bar's outer lounge. He also wrote a book on tracking, based on his experience growing up in the north country. His daughter, Connie, and wife, Ruth, run the restaurant and bar while LaHa talks hunting to his regular cronies and amazed guests. Alice Mumford is cook, whipping up such heavy-duty meals as Art's Hungry Man Steak, which weighs in between two and three pounds of prime meat ($11.95), along with homemade soup and bread. LaHa was once a butcher, so he knows his meat cuts. LaHa's is a favorite place to stop on the way to Indianhead and Big Powderhorn ski areas about 18 or so miles to the north.

Charlotte and Don Melzer, owners of the **Chicago Pub,** are dyed-in-the-wool Chicago Bears fans. That's a natural because they moved from Chicago to Winchester to raise their family in 1977. In the winter, snuggling up to the roaring fire in the pub's open fireplace is better than a visit to a tropical isle. Next door, Dick and Dorothy Hassberg of **D & D's** serve up exceptional homemade-from-the-crust-up pizza. It's the best in the Far North, according to the town's in-crowd.

Jim and Foxy Demuth hold sway at the **Star Lake Saloon and Eatery** on Highway K, 19 miles northwest of Eagle River. The red-painted saloon is one of the few buildings in the town. Their jukebox in the corner of the saloon has the best selection of Loretta Lynn country-western tunes that can be found north of Nashville. Foxy (her real name is Barbaralee) makes her own salad dressings and has a finesse with prime rib that's really unmatched. She learned to cook while the couple were stationed in France when Jim was in the military. Foxy picked up her nickname as a CB radio moniker when her husband was an overland trucker.

I discovered the place in the middle of winter a few years ago, dropping in with some friends for breakfast. Here is what we each got: a pan-fried steak, two eggs, all the juice and coffee we could drink, all the homemade powdermilk biscuits and jam we wanted, plus Foxy's special French toast (you will have to buy the saloon in order to get the recipe, she warns).

Don't get the wrong idea if I mention **Hintz's North Star Lodge** (715–542–3600) in Star Lake. We are not related to Bill Hintz, the young guy who purchased the old resort in 1984, but we've spent some pleasant vacation hours there. Daughter Kate and middle son Steve still talk about the frog-jumping contest they organized on the patio to the rear of the main building. Son Dan and wife Sandy reeled in enough fish to keep us in brain food for the entire week. I read, loafed, swam, and sunburned for a glorious seven days.

The place was built in 1894 as a retreat for railroad and lumber magnates and their guests. Bill does his own cooking, which includes fresh walleye and regular weekday specials. While we usually ate in our own cabin, we tried his Sunday brunch, a table-groaner that included homemade sweet rolls, eggs, sausage, bacon, pancakes, chicken, fried potatoes, dessert, and a ton of salads and other fixings. The eleven cabins at North Star Lodge range from $350 to $895 per week, sleeping from four to eight persons.

Not far from Star Lake is Sayner, home of the ◆ **Vilas County Historical Museum,** open daily from 10:00 A.M. through the autumn color season. The free museum has an extensive collection of old and contemporary snowmobiles, able to be seen in the winter through picture windows in the rear of the facility. The lighted display opens up to a snowmobile track that runs behind the building, so visitors can have a look even during a nighttime jaunt.

The world's first commercial snowmobile was built by the late Carl Eliason of Sayner, whose family now runs the hardware store and lumberyard across the street from the museum. In 1924 he used a small gasoline motor—attached to a long toboggan mounted on front and rear tracks—to help him get through the drifts. The idea caught on so well that now the snowmobile is the north land's main form of winter recreational transportation. The prototypes of Eliason's vehicles are in the exhibit.

The annual Snowmobile World Championship Derby is always a big affair in Eagle River, celebrating its thirty-second anniversary in 1995. On the third weekend each January, pro racers flock to the track that has been coated with 16 inches of solid ice. Speeds over 100 mph have been clocked on the half-mile banked oval. For information and ticket prices about upcoming derbies, call (715) 479–4424.

The complex is owned by Audrey and Dick Decker, a lively couple who also run Deckers' Sno-Venture Tours. They have taken snowmobile riders to Finland, Iceland, Canada, Yosemite, and other exotic locales, as well as on lengthy trips around northern Wisconsin and into the Upper Peninsula of Michigan. A Decker tour is something special, bonding a disparate group of folks of all riding skills who come from around the country. The Deckers also put together special packages for corporate groups, providing long, challenging rides to CEOs and their staffs who want a different sort of getaway from the office.

Some of the best memories I had on a recent five-day Decker trip from Eagle River to Bayfield and back again were the roasted hot dogs in a warming cabin in Chequamegon Forest, grouse exploding out of the thickets near Iron River, and the sight of the vast frozen waters of Lake Superior just before the sun came up. For details on tours, write to the Deckers at Box 1447, Eagle River 54521.

Gangsters led by bank robber John Dillinger once paused at the **Little Bohemia Resort,** near Manitowish Waters 20 miles north of Minocqua on Highway 51. In 1934 the thugs were escaping from a holdup in Racine and made it to Little Bohemia for a rest stop. Apparently it was the only place open between Mercer and Minocqua, so the gang stayed for a long weekend.

Acting on a tip, the police arrived to smoke out the notorious crew. By the time the gunfire was over, three locals who had been sitting at the bar were shot dead, and several sobbing girlfriends had been left behind by the gang. The thugs had hightailed it into the woods and escaped. The current owner, Emil Wanatka Jr., is the son of the man who operated Little Bohemia when Dillinger checked in—and out.

It's much quieter these days, but you can still see a small building on the restaurant grounds that contains items abandoned by the criminals, including underwear, some tins of laxatives, and other odds and ends.

The building itself is peppered with about one hundred bullet holes. Little Bohemia (715–543–8433) is open from mid-April to early January. From Memorial Day to Labor Day, lunches are offered from 11:30 A.M. to 2:00 P.M. and suppers from 5:00 P.M. to 10:00 P.M. The restaurant is closed Wednesdays.

Part of Woodruff lies in Oneida County, but the bulk of the community and its neighbor Arbor Vitae are on the southern edge of Vilas County. The crossroads towns share a common school district, with the main grade school in Woodruff. On the playground a block west of Highway 51 is a giant concrete penny. The town claims it is the world's largest coin, weighing in at 17,452 pounds and standing 10 feet tall. The statue was erected in 1957, recalling a fund-raiser for the local hospital that brought in a million-plus pennies. In 1952 kids in Otto Burich's geometry class wanted to see a million of something. So he suggested they count a million pennies and contribute the money as a kick-off donation for a clinic.

The medical facility was long sought by Dr. Kate Newcomb, the "Angel on Snowshoes," who delivered babies by the bushel-basket throughout the county regardless of the weather. Newcomb appeared on the old "This is Your Life" television program and told about the fund-raising efforts. Naturally, that led to more donations and the eventual construction of a clinic. Several years later, an uncle of actress Elizabeth Taylor gave the community more funds with which to build a larger medical unit. He had vacationed in the Woodruff–Arbor Vitae area for years and wanted to help the towns.

**87**

Woodruff celebrated its centennial in 1988, with a re-creation of the first **Penny Parade,** the one launching the children's efforts three decades earlier. Dr. Newcomb's refurbished home on Second Street, just around the corner from the school and the giant penny, was also opened as a museum.

Log rolling, wood chopping, and tree climbing are a few of the events presented on the grounds of **Scheer's Lumberjack Show** (715–356–4050) in downtown Woodruff. The program of logger skills is open from mid-June through late August. Tickets are $4.50 for adults and $3.00 for youngsters. Fred Scheer, a world champion log roller, his brother Bob, a record holder in pole climbing, and their sister Judy, the seven-time world's record holder in women's log rolling, form the core of the entertainers' troupe. Other family members and professional loggers also demonstrate their timber talents during shows at 2:00 and 7:00 P.M. Monday through Saturday.

## WASHBURN COUNTY

The world's largest warm-water fish hatchery in the world, according to the Wisconsin Department of Natural Resources which runs the place, is located in Spooner. The sprawling facility is south of downtown on Highway 63, across two bridges.

The DNR has a nice picnic area on the grounds, where you can put up your feet and watch the fingerlings splish and splash. Several varieties of game fish are raised here for stocking North Woods lakes. It's enough to want to bring a fishing pole.

# EASTERN WISCONSIN

1. Oneida Nation Museum
2. Green Bay Packer Hall of Fame
3. Blue Heron Landing
4. J.W. Jung Seed Company
5. Washington Island
6. Rock Island
7. Walleye Weekend
8. Emma Carlin Hiking Trail
9. Aztalan State Park
10. Hoard Historical Museum and Dairy Exhibit
11. Bristol Renaissance Faire
12. Von Stiehl Winery
13. Manitowoc Maritime Museum
14. Beerntsen's Candies
15. Point Beach State Forest
16. Outagamie Museum
17. Houdini Plaza
18. Pioneer Village
19. World's Largest One-Day Outdoor Fish Fry
20. Hobo's Korner Kitchen
21. Golden Rondelle
22. Beloit College
23. Logan Museum of Anthropology
24. Tallman Restorations
25. Rock Aqua Jays
26. Kettle Moraine Vineyards
27. Clown Hall of Fame
28. St. Patrick's Day parade
29. Old World Wisconsin
30. Southern Kettle Moraine Forest
31. Olympia Spa
32. Chain O'Lakes
33. Experimental Aircraft Association Fly-in

# EASTERN WISCONSIN

The eastern portion of Wisconsin near Lake Michigan has the greatest concentration of population in the state, but there are still secret treasures of travel waiting there for you. For an extensive overview of what the nation's inland coast has to offer, take the Lake Michigan Circle Tour. For 1,000 miles, the route carries tourists through Wisconsin, Michigan, Indiana, and Illinois. Wisconsin's 300-mile connection begins at Highway 32 south of Kenosha and concludes at Highway 41 in Marinette. Many lakeshore towns have designated "spur" routes off the main Circle drive, to show off their home neighborhoods.

The route is marked by 3x3-foot green-and-white signs set about every 5 miles. In most areas, the route meanders close to city beaches, harbors, and marinas, so be sure to bring a fishing pole and suntan lotion. Angling licenses can be secured at most bait and tackle shops, so don't let the initial lack of the right paperwork be an impediment.

For your reference, here's the Wisconsin leg of the Circle route: Highway 32 through Kenosha, Racine, Milwaukee, and Port Washington to its interchange with Interstate 43 north of Port Washington; Interstate 43 to the interchange with Highway 42 southwest of Sheboygan; Highway 42 through Sheboygan to the junction with Interstate 43 northwest of Sheboygan; I–43 to its interchange with Highway 151 southwest of Manitowoc.

Take Highway 151 to downtown Manitowoc, then to Highway 10 and its junction with Highway 42 north of the downtown. Drive Highway 42 through Two Rivers, Kewaunee, and Algoma to Sturgeon Bay; Highway 57 up the east side of Door County to Sister Bay; Highway 42 down the east shore of Green Bay back to Sturgeon Bay.

Then move on Highway 57 to its junction with Highway 29 in Green Bay; Highway 29 through downtown Green Bay to its interchange with Highway 41 in Howard; take Highway 41 west along the shore of Green Bay to Marinette and the Michigan border.

You'll go through communities in Kenosha, Racine, Milwaukee, Ozaukee, Sheboygan, Manitowoc, Kewanee, Door, Brown, Oconto, and Marinette counties on your Circle adventure. En route, you'll hit restaurants, museums, lodgings, and other attractions that blend in perfectly with the lakefront milieu.

# BROWN COUNTY

The ◆ **Oneida Nation Museum** in De Pere, a Green Bay suburb, offers keen insights into the lives of this Native American tribe, which came to Wisconsin in the 1820s. There's a hands-on room in which kids can play a drum and try on an eagle feather headdress. The museum is located at the intersection of Highways E and EE. It's open from 9:00 A.M. to 5:00 P.M. Tuesday through Friday and from 10:00 A.M. to 2:00 P.M. Saturday and Sunday; closed Monday. Call (414) 869–2768 for more details. The tribe also operates a giant bingo parlor and casino adjacent to its Raddison Hotel across from the airport in Green Bay.

The De Pere Historical Society maintains **White Pillars,** the state's first bank building. The structure, located at 403 N. Broadway, was built in 1836 to house the currency and records of the De Pere Hydraulic Company. The firm was then building a dam across the Fox River in De Pere. Over the generations, the old bank building was alternately a barbershop, an Episcopalian meetinghouse, and a newspaper office before becoming a home. It was returned to its original look in 1973. The bank is open from 1:00 to 5:00 P.M. Wednesday through Sunday or by special appointment (414–336–3877 or 414–336–6113). Admission is free.

While in Green Bay, don't miss the ◆ **Green Bay Packer Hall of Fame,** across from Lambeau Field on Lombardi Avenue. The museum, open from 10:00 A.M. to 5:00 P.M. daily year-round, is a testimonial to all the players who have worn the gold and green of the city's pro football team over the years. You can even try kicking your own field goal there. In July and August, the team has practice sessions open to the public in the nearby stadium. A giant statue of a ball-grabbing Packer atop a football stands on the lawn in front of the museum building, in case you didn't notice the signage. Call (414) 499–4281 for details. Admission is charged to the museum.

The **National Railroad Museum,** just off Highway 41, is a nationally known train museum. While train buffs may already be aware of the history of its rolling stock, the rest of us might not be as knowledgeable. One locomotive on display, called "Big Boy," weighs in at 600 tons and is 133 feet long. Another engine pulled General Dwight Eisenhower's command train in World War II.

**91**

For details on the railroad museum, call (414) 435–7245. The facility is open daily year-round from 9:00 A.M. to 5:00 P.M. From May 1 through October 15, train rides are offered at 10:00 and 11:30 A.M. and at 2:30 and 4:00 P.M. Summer admission is $6.00 for adults, $5.00 for seniors (sixty-two and over), $3.00 for youngsters six through fifteen, and free for kids five and under. An immediate family rate is $16.00 (two adults and all kids under eighteen). During the winter season, October 15 through April 30, admission is generally half price because the train ride is not available.

For eating, **Chili John's** is famous for its namesake food, ranging from spicy enough to curl hair to milder versions for daisyweights. The place has been in the same family for three generations. It's located at 519 S. Military Avenue in the Beacon Shopping Center (414–494–4624), at the intersection of Highway 54. Takeouts are available. Some wags claim you can use the hottest version for fueling a motorboat, but don't believe 'em. Just eat and be satisfied.

## Dodge County

Dodge County is rich in farmland, layered with rolling hills and spotted with lakes. Westford, Mud Lake, Shaw Marsh, Theresa Marsh, and Horicon Marsh wildlife areas and the Horicon National Wildlife Refuge, as well as Fox, Emily, Beaver Dam, and Sinissippi lakes, are the county's pride and joy. Outdoors fans flock here regardless of the season for bird-watching, hunting, fishing, or just plain loafing.

Our favorite canoeing jaunt is deep into the Horicon refuge, angling for bullheads and watching for blue herons and sandhill cranes. The wildlife refuge has several large rookeries of each, accessible only by water. The ◆**Blue Heron Landing,** near the Highway 33 bridge over the Rock River, has canoe rentals April through September and pontoon boat tours from May through the end of September.

Call (414) 485–2942 (winter) or (414) 485–4663 (summer) for details. Public boat launching sites are located at River Bend Park below the Horicon Dam in town, Ice House Slough off Chestnut Street, Arndt Ditch Landing off Highway E northwest of Horicon, and Burnett Ditch Landing on the west side of the marsh.

If you have kids too little to take into the marsh, let them fish for bullheads from the grassy west side riverbank across from the John Deere plant, near the Highway 33 bridge west of downtown. Pubs in the neighborhood offer pickled eggs and pig's feet, two gourmet treats for the macho set.

Canada geese use the county's cornfields and swamps for a regular autumn pit stop on their way south. They fly from the Hudson Bay in Canada to their winter layover where the Ohio River joins the Mississippi. Up to 100,000, sometimes more, birds are counted in the marsh each year. Subsequently, on some weekends, traffic is bumper to bumper along the county roads ringing the marshes as rubberneckers strain to see the giant fowl. Some of the feathered fliers weigh in at an impressive eighteen pounds or more, with a wingspread of 6 feet. If you can, take a middle-of-the-week jaunt around the Horicon instead of a Saturday or Sunday run. You'll be able to stop and stare to your heart's content at the sky-blackening flocks without worrying about backed-up traffic.

The town celebrates its link with the environment during Horicon Marsh Days in July, with activities ranging from street sales to a drum and bugle corps competition that attracts groups from around southeastern Wisconsin. In September, the Autumn Art on the Marsh show is held in Discher Park, on Cedar Street. The show provides an opportunity to stock up on Christmas presents.

Founded in 1907, the ❖**J. W. Jung Seed Company** in Randolph is another Dodge County attraction, located 40 miles northeast of Madison. Each winter, while planning for planting, gardeners eagerly look forward to the company's nationally distributed mail-order vegetable and flower catalogs. The firm prints its own catalogs, up to 2.5 million copies a year, with 5,000 orders for seeds and plantings per day during the peak spring season. Few people realize that tours of Jung are available if you call ahead (414–326–3121). There's also the opportunity for green thumbers to stop in at the company's garden store, open from 8:00 A.M. to 5:00 P.M. Monday through Friday and from 8:00 A.M. to 2:00 P.M. Saturday. It sells shrubs, evergreens, seeds, fruit trees, and plants.

Specialists are on hand to answer questions about plantings, soil conditions, and all those similar tough details that are necessary to help create the perfect vegetable or flower garden. To ensure the continuation of its fine stock, the company has test plots for many varieties of plants, from gladioluses to seed corn.

The firm's founder, J. W. Jung, died in 1988 at age one hundred. Even after he had hit the century mark, however, Jung was often out speaking to his customers, spending a full day at work. The company currently is run by grandson Richard Zondag and other members of the family.

The **Dodge County Fairgrounds** in Beaver Dam has stock car races each Saturday night, with time trials at 7:00 P.M. and the first race at 8:00 P.M. The track is 3 miles east of Beaver Dam on Highway 33.

For a quieter, but a buzzing good time, there's the **Honey of a Museum** on Highway 67, 2 miles north of Ashippun. More than two million pounds of honey are produced each year at the apiary located there. Spigots in the museum allow you to taste the different flavors of honey, from tart wildflower to bitter brown buckwheat and smooth golden clover. Honey is sold in a shop on the grounds, with numerous varieties from plain to that spiced with apricot bits. The museum (414–474–4411) is open from 9:00 A.M. to 3:30 P.M. Monday through Friday and from noon to 4:00 P.M. Saturday and Sunday from May 15 to the end of October. Admission is free.

Ashippun is also a regular launch site for Balloons Unlimited. Flights take off just after sunrise or just before sunset. I took my wife, Sandy, on a birthday flight, meeting in the dim morning at the Firemen's Park on the west side of town, near the baseball field. The ascension was to be a surprise; we rolled out of bed at 4:30 A.M. to be sure we made it to the launching on time.

The balloon operators always call around that unholy hour to let you know if the trip is on or not, after carefully checking the weather and wind conditions. The pilots are FAA certified. The trip took off on schedule, drifting over the Dodge and Waukesha county landscape and providing an entirely different perspective of Alderly, Monches, Mapleton, North Lake, Chenequa, and Hartland. Dogs barked and people waved at our silent flight as we drifted along. I remember crossing one of the small lakes near County Road K and seeing the reflection of the red and yellow balloon dancing across the calm surface of the water. It was like another world. For information about the flights, contact Balloons Unlimited at (414) 593–8961. Cost for the two-hour flight is $180 per person. Upon landing, you are presented with a balloonist certificate, a T-shirt, and pin.

# DOOR COUNTY

Door County has often been called the Cape Cod of Wisconsin. The rocky coast juts like a thumb into the frosty waters of Lake Michigan, separating the lake from Green Bay. It's a harsh landscape, one that artists love. Scandinavian farmers and fishers settled the vicinity, appreciating its environmental kinship of their homeland. We like the county regardless of the season. Spring has the fragrance of cherry and apple blossoms. Summer's hard heat is beaten only in the cool woods or by swimming.

We just wish that some of the small towns were not becoming so commercialized, with what appears to us an overabundance of minimalls featuring crafts, candles, ribbons, and trendy hiking wear. All these shops have become too much of a good thing. So we prefer to hit the backroads where it's more relaxing.

Autumn's colorama in Door County is considered among the best in the state. A drive around the peninsula in October provides the last opportunity to scour the county's antique shops before they close for the snowbound winter. Winter? Well, there's cross-country skiing, followed by a huddle in front of the fireplace with a hot toddy.

The city of Sturgeon Bay is the entry point for the county, where Highways 42 and 57 link to cross the ship channel. To get there any other way, you'll have to swim, sail, or fly; all of which are excellent options, of course, if you have your own fins, yacht, or plane. Regardless of the transport mode, the county has facilities to accommodate anyone's arrival.

Door County is noted for its many excellent inns and guest houses. Among the best in Sturgeon Bay are the White Lace Inn, 16 N. Fifth Street (414–743–1105), the Bay Shore Inn, 4205 Bay Shore Drive (414–743–4551), the Inn at Cedar Crossing, 336 Louisiana (414–743–4200), and the Scofield House, 908 Michigan (414–743–7727). In Ephraim, try the French Country Inn, 30 Spruce Lane (414–854–4001).

The Griffin Inn, 11976 Mink River Road, Ellison Bay (414–854–4306), and the White Apron Inn, 414 Maple Drive, Sister Bay (414–854–5107), are two other excellent lodgings on the peninsula. One of the most popular in Door County is Jan and Andy Coulson's White Gull Inn, Box 159, Fish Creek (414–868–3517).

## White Apron Inn

Hospitality and moderate pricing are the name of the game for all these accommodations.

Of all the Door County traditions, the fish boil is the most famous. Almost every roadside restaurant and inn offers some version of this popular summer "event." The chef boils a huge pot of water over an outside blaze, tossing in Bunyan-sized hunks of Lake Michigan whitefish, which are then left to simmer for hours. For the next step, salt, seasonings, onions, and potatoes are added to give it punch. No eyes of newt or wing of bat are needed—this is your basic stick-to-the-ribs food. The water is then heated to boiling, pouring over the rim of a pot in a vast plume of steam. The boil carries off all the fats with the scalding foam.

You can then sit down for a breeze-touched picnic. Add home-made bread and jam, plenty of fresh garden vegetables, a piece of apple pie topped with Wisconsin vanilla ice cream, and a beer or two or fresh-ground coffee—there's a real feast, worth getting off the state's beaten path.

◆**Washington Island** is reached only by ferry from the Gills Rock on the Door County mainland. The island has been discovered by tourists, which has led to an overabundance of gift shops near the harbor mouth. But once you get away from the ferry landing, the island is delightfully pretty. Spend a day driving around the island backroads or rent a bike at the dockside. We were running late during one vacation exploration and had to catch the night's last ferryboat. With about a minute to spare, Sandy, who has delusions of Grand Prix racing, got us from the north end of the island to the south end. I don't recommend a careening drive like that on a regular basis because the roads are too twisting and narrow. But at least we made the boat landing in time.

◆ **Rock Island** is the next island out from Washington, also reached only by ferryboat. No cars are allowed in this state park, so be prepared to hike. Without the noise of autos to compete with the surf and the wind rustling the beech leaves, you can spot the deer and other wildlife that live on the craggy spit of rock and sand. Pack a lunch and sit on the north beach looking out over the lake. The view is tremendous. Archaeologists have been poking around the island for several years, discovering ancient Indian villages and burial places, as well as checking out abandoned pioneer settlements. The sites are well marked, but don't go around digging on your own. They're all legally protected.

## FOND DU LAC COUNTY

Ripon proudly struts the fact that the Republican Party was formed here when a group of disgruntled politicians met on March 20, 1854. The building in which they got together is now called the **Little White Schoolhouse.** The building on Blackburn Street is open daily throughout the summer and early autumn.

The city of Fond du Lac is on the southern rim of Lake Winnebago, with a large white lighthouse at the Lakeside Park to act as a focal point for outdoor events. The city's ◆ **Walleye Weekend** each June attracts anglers from all over the Midwest to compete for cash prizes and the adulation of fellow fishing fanatics. The folks claim that they have the world's largest fish fry on that weekend. For details call the Fond du Lac Convention and Visitors Bureau, (414) 923–3010 or (800) 937–9123.

## JEFFERSON COUNTY

The ◆**Emma Carlin Hiking Trail** is one of the state's best, beginning in a parking lot on County Trunk Z, south of Highway 59 only 2 miles east of Palmyra. The trail offers three loops of varying distance, with a pond, meadows, and plenty of wildlife. Eagles are often spotted high in the air over the aspen and basswood groves that are scattered between the oak stands. Sometimes, turkey vultures can be seen swooping and soaring overhead as well.

After a brisk hike on the trail, indulge in all the creature comforts at the **Fargo Mansion Inn** (414–648–3654) in Lake Mills. Enoch Fargo, a descendant of the stagecoach family, built the home at the turn of the century. It became the town's social center, complete with towers, woodwork, lavish foyer, and huge kitchen with a walk-in freezer. The neighbors were amazed when Fargo put in a cement sidewalk out front, supposedly the first in Wisconsin.

After a succession of owners, including one family that hosted eighty foster children (over the years, not all at once), the building was listed on the National Register of Historic Places in 1982 and made into a guest house in 1986. Five bedrooms are on the second floor, reached by a staircase worthy of Cinderella. The rooms are named for former occupants of the mansion. Another four to five suites have been added to the building's third floor by owner Barry Luce and his partner Tom Boycks.

The inn has tandem bikes for use in the summer, for pedaling along the nearby Glacial Drumlin Trail. Prices at the inn are moderate and include a continental breakfast.

Near Lake Mills is ◆**Aztalan State Park** and the southern unit of Kettle Moraine Forest. On the summer weekends, dirt bike racers zoom near the park on a twisted, turning motocross track that can be seen from Interstate 94. Their roaring engines, however, can't be heard at the site of a prehistoric village to the south. The tribe that settled here was thought to be an outpost of ancient mound builders who lived in southern Illinois.

Artifacts found throughout the region show that the inhabitants were great traders. Shells, precious metals, and implements not indigenous to central Wisconsin have been found in farm fields and along riverbanks. The artifacts and pioneer tools are displayed at the **Lake Mills–Aztalan Historical Society Museum,**

3 miles east of Lake Mills on County Trunk B. Several log cabins are on the museum site, open from 10:00 A.M. to 5:00 P.M., May through mid-October. For information call (414) 648–5872. Donations are requested.

The state has erected a palisade where the village once stood, similar to one that archaeologists say protected the tribespeople from marauding enemy bands. Excellent markers and signage around the grounds tell the story of the Aztalan tribe. A picnic site is nearby at the foot of a hill leading down to a creek. On one of our excursions there, the kids spent a half day fishing after reading how the Indians used the same waterway for their fish traps and netting. It is possible that this community was somehow related to the Cahokia Mounds people of southwestern Illinois. Archaeologists have discovered many similar artifacts and building styles at both sites.

Fort Atkinson is home of the ◆ **Hoard Historical Museum and Dairy Exhibit,** 407 Merchants Avenue (414–563–7769). The museum is open year-round from 9:30 A.M. to 5:00 P.M. Tuesday through Saturday and from 1:00 to 5:00 P.M. on the first Sunday of the month. The exhibits trace the developments of the American dairy industry, with plaques honoring famous scientists and dairy operators. Fort Atkinson has long been famous as a dairy and agricultural publishing center where such important magazines as *Hoard's Dairyman* are produced.

The Hoard Museum also traces the action of the U.S. Army and militia in the Black Hawk War of 1832. Several skirmishes took place in Jefferson County between pursuing troops and their quarry, the Fox and allies who were led by the famed warrior Black Hawk.

Young Abraham Lincoln was one of the militiamen who chased the Indians to the Mississippi River, where they were massacred while trying to escape by swimming across. A large map in the museum shows where soldiers and Indians camped as they jockeyed back and forth.

The town also has a replica of Fort Koshkonong, originally built to protect settlers during the Black Hawk War. An outdoor drama entitled *Black Hawk* is staged here each August, featuring about one hundred local performers.

Nearby are several prehistoric Indian markers, one of which resembles a huge panther. That intaglio (design cut into the surface of the earth) was probably constructed around A.D. 1000.

The Fort Atkinson form is believed to be one of only two such earthworks remaining in the world (another intaglio in the shape of a panther is in Ontario). The design is rare, because most of the patterns made by the Indians were in mounds, rather than in depressions in the ground. The intaglio is located on the west bank of the Rock River, on Highway 106 at the west edge of town. Actually, you will have to use your imagination in "seeing" the beast, because at least 25 feet of the tail was destroyed by construction of a driveway in 1941. The depression is grass-covered, near some hedges and sidewalks at 1236 Riverside Drive.

On Highway 26 on the south side of town is the **Fireside Playhouse** and restaurant (414–563–9505), which stages live theater-in-the-round productions, many of which are well-known musicals. The theater is popular with tour groups. The country's top folk and acoustic musicians perform regularly at the **Café Carp,** a club operated by well-known singer Bill Camplin and co-owner Kitty Welch at 18 S. Water Street West (414–563–9391). Not quite a throwback to the coffeehouse days of the 1960s, but it's close enough. The Café Carp has a soothing ambience and good vibes, a place to call a musical home.

In Watertown, on the county's north side, is the restored building that was the nation's first kindergarten. A German teacher, Margarethe Meyer Schurz, brought this form of teaching youngsters to the United States in 1856. The structure was originally in downtown Watertown but was moved to the site of the **Octagon House museum** in 1956. Both museums are open daily from 11:00 A.M. to 3:00 P.M. from May 1 to November 1 (919 Charles Street, 414–261–2796). Admission is $3.00 for adults; $1.00 for students six to seventeen; and $2.50 for seniors and AAA members. Kids five and under get in free.

While in Watertown, stop for ice cream at **Mullen's Dairy Bar** on West Main Street (414–261–4278). The dairy still produces its own creamery products. Scattered around the room are old advertising materials, glass milk bottles, and similar items from the company's past.

## KENOSHA COUNTY

Kenosha County is tucked into the far southeastern corner of the state, where Lake Michigan laps along its miles of beach frontage.

The rolling waters provided opportunities for trade and fishing, so pioneer settlers plunked down their log cabins along the shoreline. Eventually, a string of mansions grew up along the lakeside, especially in Kenosha, the county seat. They include the **Kemper Center,** once a girls' school, renovated as a conference center at 6501 Third Avenue (414–657–6005); **Harmony Hall,** 6315 Third Avenue, now the headquarters of the Society for the Preservation and Encouragement of Barbershop Quartet Singing in America (free tours are offered there from 10:00 A.M. to 3:00 P.M. daily during the summer); the Manor House bed and breakfast and lecture center, 6536 Third Avenue (414–658–0014); and the **Kenosha County Historical Society Museum,** 6399 Third Avenue (414–654–5770).

If gazing at older buildings isn't your forte, perhaps fishing is. The county boasts the largest catch rate of coho salmon and lake trout of any along the Wisconsin side of Lake Michigan. Coho-rama, a celebration of that fabled fighting fish, is usually held in mid-June and features a fishing contest . . . what else?

For great eating, try the homemade goodies at **The Cooper House,** 2227 60th Street (414–657–9314). Pies, cakes, and other delights round off a full American menu.

The primo hamburger joint in town is **Ron's Place,** 3301 52nd Street (414–657–5907). It's inexpensive, with a delicious half-pound burger called the "5x5" that is guaranteed to show up any national fast-food chain's poor excuse for a sandwich. Without fries, the 5x5 is only $2.90. With fries, it's $3.60. Ron's has other eats as well, of course, but when it comes to burgers, I won't eat anywhere else in Kenosha.

The ◆ **Bristol Renaissance Faire** in Bristol Township is a fun step way, way back into history. Jugglers, whipcrackers, trou-badours, poets, and minstrels put on shows during July and August weekends. The eighty-acre site is near the Illinois-Wisconsin border just off Interstate 94. From Chicago, take Interstate 94 West to Highway 41 north, exit at Russell Road.

From Milwaukee, take Interstate 94 East, exit at County Road V and follow the Frontage Road. There's usually a College of Wizards, bawdy comedy, games of skill (get the kids to slay a dragon), and a sword fight or two. For tickets, contact the Faire, (414–396–4320).

For more traditional entertainment, there's the Kenosha Twins baseball team (the Minnesota Twins farm club), which plays on

Simmons Field. For ticket prices and dates, contact the team offices at 7817 Sheridan Road, Kenosha 53140 (414–657–7997). The pro team is a member of the Class A Midwest League, funneling players into the majors. The club has a chicken mascot that roams the infield looking for action, carrying its baseball bat and a mitt. No, it's not a real chicken naturally, but a kid dressed as one.

The community is in the process of expanding its marina, a building project that will take several years. Lake Michigan boaters can find some of the best berthing facilities along the Wisconsin side in Kenosha, complete with changing rooms for weekend sailors who wish to slip into their nautical gear straight from work. Already in place are a fuel and sanitary pump-out pier, lift-out well, and jib crane, along with more restroom and shower facilities.

## KEWAUNEE COUNTY

Algoma is a photographer's dream on early summer mornings, especially as the state's largest charter fishing fleet sets out from the harbor. The city claims record lake salmon catches every year just offshore. Who's to argue when boat after boat returns with hefty catches after a full day on the choppy Lake Michigan waters? It's not uncommon to haul in twenty-pound chinook off Algoma Shores.

◈ **Von Stiehl Winery** at 115 Navarino Street in Algoma (414–487–5208) is open for tours daily from May through October. Perusing the collection of toy trolls on display is almost as much fun as visiting the sampling room. The winery specializes in sweet and semisweet wines and has won several national and international awards.

The city hosts an annual Doll Show in July, in which dealers from around the country come to show off antique and contemporary dolls, as well as all the accessories—just the thing for kids. The event is held in Knudsen Hall and Youth Center, 620 Lake Street.

Kewaunee County can promise dolls, wine, and huge fish. It can also show off the world's largest grandfather clock, located on Kewaunee's north side. The old timepiece, which stands 35 feet tall, is the trademark of the Svoboda Industries (414–388–2691), a one-hundred-year-old firm that specializes in all sorts of wood products. The clock is on the facade of the factory, chiming every fifteen minutes. The Svoboda plant is located on Highways 42 and 29, making smaller versions of the grandfather clock, in addition to furniture, carvings, and other wooden household accessories.

## MANITOWOC COUNTY

The county fronts the rolling waters of Lake Michigan, with a string of towns along the shore that look like diamonds when their lights sparkle at night. The coastline, although lost in darkness, glimmers when putt-putting along in a powerboat. The best view is from a half mile or so offshore on a lazy summer evening.

The city of Manitowoc must be one of the few towns that has its own submarine. The USS *Cobia,* acquired by the ◆**Manitowoc Maritime Museum** from the U.S. Navy in 1970, has been outfitted just as it was during combat in World War II. Recorded battle sounds, accurate to the shouts of "dive, dive, dive," lend reality to the tight quarters. The 311-foot-long vessel had a distinguished career, sinking thirteen Japanese vessels in 1944 and 1945. After decommissioning, the sub was assigned as a training ship for Milwaukee's submarine reserves unit. Manitowoc secured the *Cobia* as a memorial to the factory workers who built twenty-eight subs in city plants during the war.

The museum itself celebrates life on Lake Michigan, with exhibits of shipwrecks, model vessels, diving gear, photographs, and artifacts. It opened in 1969 but moved to new quarters in 1986, a building complete with a "street" that includes a ship chandlery, port office, and other storefronts.

One of the most interesting displays is a full-scale section of a sailing ship as it would have appeared during construction in 1854. The beams, spikes, and caulking are all in their proper places, detailing the intricate work that went into the rugged lake vessels.

The museum (414–684–0218) is located at 75 Maritime Drive, in downtown Manitowoc. It is open from 9:00 A.M. to 5:00 P.M. daily all year. Admission is charged.

The **Inn on Maritime Bay** (414–682–7000) is the place to eat in Manitowoc, featuring fish and steak. If you come with a crowd or are especially hungry, order a hunk of sugar-cured champagne ham (at $65 to feed forty hearty eaters) or a steamship round of beef ($250 for one hundred persons). General menu prices, of course, are moderate. The inn is on the shore in downtown Manitowoc and offers short "getaways" such as the Waterfront Retreat and Castaway Package. The latter includes a box lunch for fishing or sailing, two of the most popular sports in town.

Speaking of eating, it's obvious that no one need ever go hungry in Manitowoc, especially when strolling into ◆ **Beerntsen's Candies** at 108 N. Eighth Street (414) 684–9616. This tiny shop with its soda fountain has been a tradition in the city since, well, let's say when chocolate was invented. Homemade temptations line the shelves in all their caloric splendor. Beerntsen's hot fudge is so lusciously thick and rich, it makes a lava flow look like skim milk. Hours are 10:00 A.M. to 10:00 P.M. daily year-round.

Mishicot is the Indian term for "place of shelter," tucked into farmland at the junction of Highways 147 and 163. Lake Michigan is about 10 miles to the east. **River Edge Galleries** (414–755–4777) has one of the most extensive collections of Wisconsin fine artists of any state showplace, regularly displaying Guido Brink, Patrick Farrell, and other state personalities. The two-story gallery on the East Twin River is located at 432 East Main Street.

The **Point Beach Nuclear Power Plant,** operated by the Wisconsin Electric Power Company, stabs the skyline north of Two Rivers off Highway 42. The plant neither glows in the dark nor conjures images of disaster. In fact, it is one of eastern Wisconsin's least-known educational sites. The facility's Energy Information Center is open daily from 8:30 A.M. to 5:00 P.M. April to October and from 10:00 A.M. to 4:30 P.M. November through March. Admission is free.

The information center is stocked with computers that let kids—and grownups—play games with energy. You can tour a model nuclear reactor and see how a Geiger counter measures radiation in ordinary items found around a house. Movies, slides, and tapes on energy topics can be viewed at the center. There's even a half-mile marked nature trail with signs explaining the energy cycle and interdependence of animal and plant life.

If coming north on Interstate 43, take exit 79 to Manitowoc and follow Highway 42 to the plant entrance. From the north, take exit 91 to Mishicot and follow Highway 163 to Nuclear Road where signs will direct you to the information center entrance. For information on programs at the center, write the plant at 6600 Nuclear Road, Two Rivers 54241 or call 414–755–4334. You can call collect outside the Two Rivers area.

❖**Point Beach State Forest** (414–794–7480) is just south of the power plant, covering more than 2,800 acres of prime timber bordered by 6 miles of sand dunes along Lake Michigan. The woods contain beech, hemlock, maple, yellow birch, and numerous other varieties of trees.

Wildlife is abundant, ranging from deer and fox to mink and muskrats. Naturalist programs are held regularly there throughout the summer. You can see the remains of several wrecked ships off Rowley Point while hiking along the beach.

The ice cream sundae was supposedly invented in Two Rivers, about 6 miles north of Manitowoc on Highway 42. On a steamy Sunday in 1881, Ed Berner, owner of a local soda fountain, was asked to top off a dish of ice cream with chocolate sauce. The sauce was usually used only for sodas, but the new concoction took off in popularity once the town's youngsters tried it. A glass vendor saw potential in the product and ordered special sets of canoe-shaped dishes for Berner, calling them sundae dishes. A plaque marking the event stands in the downtown. Berner's fountain at 1404 Fifteenth Street is gone now, replaced by a parking lot for Kurtz's Vintage Wine Cellar.

## OUTAGAMIE COUNTY

The fate and future of Outagamie County, linked to Calumet and Winnebago counties to the south, is closely tied to Lake Winnebago and the Fox River. Since pioneer times, the county has been a commercial center. The waterways brought explorers, settlers, and traders into the heart of Wisconsin from Green Bay and Lake Michigan.

The ❖**Outagamie Museum,** run by the county historical society, is different from many of its sister museums around the state. This facility concentrates on the industrial and corporate heritage of the Fox River Valley. The displays cover electricity, papermaking, financial services, agriculture, and communication, as well as local history. Tools of Change, depicting technology's impact on culture between 1840 to 1950, is fascinating. The standing exhibit is a must-see for kids, who can tour a machine shop, a doctor's office, and other "rooms" to see how various tools are used. The museum is located at 330 E. College Avenue in Appleton (414–735–9370 or 414–733–8445).

To tour Appleton, exit Highway 41 on College Avenue and park at the city ramp at the Paper Valley Hotel. Walk down the steps at Jones Park for a look at the locks and dam on the Fox River and cross the river on the Oneida Skyline Bridge. Return to the Appleton Center office building and walk through it to ◆ **Houdini Plaza,** which commemorates Appleton's famous native son, magician Harry Houdini. There is a sculpture in the plaza of the noted performer, who was born in the city in 1874 as Erich Weiss. The young man took the name of the famous French magician Houdin when he launched his career as an escape artist.

## OZAUKEE COUNTY

Take a step back one hundred years, whizzing over the crest of County Road I. The Wisconsin frontier of the 1840s pops out of the farmland at the Ozaukee County ◆ **Pioneer Village,** on the north edge of Hawthorne Hills Park.

Fifteen settlers' buildings from around the county were moved to the site and reassembled into a village, bounded by an 1860s split rail fence from the Alvin Wiskerchen farm. The rails are mostly cedar, but there are some oak and ash as well. The village is open mid-morning to early evening each Sunday and Wednesday, when curators demonstrate pioneer skills, such as log trimming, weaving, bread baking, and iron work. All the buildings are furnished in the styles from the 1840s to the early 1900s, depending on the structure.

There's nothing fishy about Port Washington, 25 miles north of Milwaukee on the shores of Lake Michigan, except that it offers excellent angling for coho and lake trout. The city has a relatively new marina, built in 1982, that has a fish cleaning station at the waterfront, plus boat launching facilities. You can also fish from the breakwater and along the piers. Keep an eye on the kids, however, because the chill lake water runs deep and fast even close to shore. Fourth of July fireworks are popped off at the marina, making a blazing spectacle over the harbor entrance.

Port Washington celebrates what it claims is the ◆ **World's Largest One-Day Outdoor Fish Fry** on the third Saturday of each July. Having attended several of these events, I'm not one to offer a challenge. You want fish, you get fish. Seemingly tons of it. Plus the usual french fried potatoes as a side delight. Fish fry aficionados love the smoked fish eating contest, an activity I prefer to pass.

The local firefighters usually have a hose war, trying with their streams of water to push a beer barrel across a wire strung between two poles. The opposing side attempts to push it back, making for a wet time for all participants. A hint: Don't stand close. The teams sometimes will playfully squirt the crowd, especially if it's a hot day.

Port Washington has several excellent restaurants specializing in fish. Among the best is **Smith Brothers Fish Shanty** on dockside. In addition to sit-down dinners (in the pricey range), a fish market there has almost any kind of finny fella—fresh— you can imagine. After a full meal, stroll down to the wharf to watch the anglers.

The city's downtown Chamber of Commerce building on Grand Avenue is called the **Pebble House.** On the National Register of Historic Places, the old home was built in Greek Revival style with rubble stone walls 20 inches thick. The foundation of the building was constructed of pebbles and rocks collected along the shoreline by original owners Elizabeth and Henry Dodge in 1848. The house was moved to its current location in 1985, pebbles and all. To reach the Chamber of Commerce, call (414) 284-0900.

The last remaining authentic covered bridge of what had been forty in the state is in Ozaukee County's **Covered Bridge County Park.** The bridge over Cedar Creek was built in 1876 and "retired" from service in 1962. You'll find the structure by going west of downtown Grafton on Highway 60, to the junction with Highway 143. Turn north there on Covered Bridge Road.

◆ **Hobo's Korner Kitchen** in Belgium (414–285–3417) is one of those truck stops where the food is plentiful, the conversation boisterous, the jukebox packed with country-western tunes. There is plenty of room to park, move, stretch, and grin. The stop is directly to the west of Highway 43, the main four-lane to Sheboygan, at exit 107. Fridays are the best times to stop if you like fish. All-you-can-eat cod is only $5.95, including fries, two slabs of bread, coleslaw, a cup of soup, and enough tartar sauce to fill a ten-gallon pail. If you want to go fancy, try the Poor Man's Lobster at $5.25, with vegetables and potatoes. In the winter, the Korner Kitchen offers hot, spiced cider.

# RACINE COUNTY

The thunder and fire of Revolutionary War Days echoes through Colonel Heg Park each June in Norway, a crossroads township in the county's northern lake district on Highway 36. Regiments belonging to the Northwest Territory Alliance turn out in force to show off their colonial or loyalist garb and recreate eighteenth-century military life. There's always a battle or two, plenty of drill demonstrations, cannon firing, and musketry. The units depict actual regiments that fought during the Revolution, with details complete to the last pewter button. The 500-plus persons who have time-warped back two centuries act out living history characters. Don't be surprised, therefore, if no one talks about life after 1780. They just haven't gotten there yet!

The hobbyists are doctors, lawyers, factory workers, homemakers, and a range of people in other professions, all of whom love the dramatic aspect of the era. My sons and I have often participated in the event, as members of the 84th Regiment of Foot, Royal Highland Emigrants (a loyalist Scots unit raised to defend Quebec at the outset of the war; a battalion of the regiment was based at northern Michigan's Fort Michilimackinac and often conducted tax-collecting missions along the Lake Michigan shoreline in Wisconsin).

The encampment at Colonel Heg Park is one of a dozen or so staged annually in the Midwestern states that make up the old Northwest Territories of pre–Revolutionary War days: Wisconsin included.

The park, however, is named after a Racine County officer of Norwegian heritage who fought for the Union during the Civil War. His statue overlooks a grove where the reenacters put on their battle demonstrations.

Speaking of Scandinavians, Racine has long been host to one of the county's largest colonies of Danish immigrants. And someday a poet will compose an ode honoring the delightful, delicious Danish kringle, the most delectable pastry of them all. Racine is the Kringle Capital of the Universe, with at least eleven bakeries where even a quick stop adds pounds to thighs and hips. The Racine Chamber of Commerce estimates that the bakeries, most of which are run by families of Danish descent, produce upwards of a million kringles annually. Many are shipped around the world for Christmas giving.

Kringles are oval-shaped layers of buttered dough, weighing about a pound and a half. They feature a variety of fillings such as pecans, walnuts, raspberry, chocolate, rhubarb, cheese, cherry, apple, custard, and even peanut butter.

Today's kringles are smaller than the 3x8-foot pastries made in nineteenth-century Denmark. Austrians taught Danish bakers the technique of layering thin sheets of butter and dough, letting the concoction sit for a day or so before flattening it with large rolling pins. Most of the initial work is still done by hand, but better rolling machines and high-tech ovens ensure easier production and consistency. Some of the large plants can make 1,500 kringles an hour, a boon during holiday time.

Stop in for a take-home munch at Bendsten's Bakery, 3200 Washington Avenue (414–633–0365), Larsen Bakery, 3311 Washington Avenue (414–633–4298), Lehmann's Bakery, 2210 16th Street (414–632–2359) or 3900 Erie Street (414–639–8748), O&H Danish Bakery, 1841 Douglas Avenue (414–637–8895 or 800–227–6665) or 4006 Durand Avenue (414–554–1311).

Yet after a generation or two in Racine, kringle making is no longer exclusively Danish. Joe Polentini Sr., of Polentini's Bakery (6100 Washington Avenue, 414–886–3392), is proud of his Italian heritage. "You don't have to be Italian to make good Italian bread," Polentini jokes.

The ◆**Golden Rondelle** at the S. C. Johnson & Son Inc. plant in Racine features several free film shows Tuesday through Friday throughout the year. They include the well-known "On the Wing," which explores the relationship between natural and mechanical flight, and "The Living Planet." Advance registrations are required, however. Contact the Guest Relations Center at the company, 1525 Howe Street, Racine 53403 (414–631–2154). The Golden Rondelle Theater was initially used by Johnson Wax at the 1964 World's Fair in New York as part of its display building.

Tours of the firm's main administration building, designed by Frank Lloyd Wright, also start at the Golden Rondelle Theater.

The Johnson company, better known as Johnson Wax, was started in 1886 as a manufacturer of parquet floors and moved into the wax business when customers asked for ways to protect their under-foot investment. Currently, the firm markets more than 200 products and carries out continuous research. A display of these items fills an exhibit room.

**109**

Burlington is proud of its reputation as home of the world-famous Burlington Liars Club, which annually hosts a competition to see who can tell the tallest tales and the biggest lies. The awards are usually given out in a local restaurant, after culling through thousands of submissions. The community also calls itself "The Chocolate City," because of its chocolate plant.

Each mid-May, the locals host a Chocolate City Festival that features a Flat Foot Run near the Nestlé Company, with 2- and 5-mile marathons.

I always stock up on chocolate whenever taking a drive along any one of the seven official Rustic Roads that grace the county. Never know when one might need a snack. Among the best tours in the state is the drive north from Burlington along Honey Lake Road, Maple Lane, and Pleasant View Road. This route eventually takes you to County Highway D and on to State Highway 83. The **Wehmhoff Woodland Preserve** on the route is a great place for muskrat watching. Another scenic backcountry expedition is along Oak Knoll Road from County Highway DD to County Highway D, adjacent to the Honey Creek Wildlife District. Wheatland Road from State Highway 142 south to Hoosier Creek Road and on to County Highway JB is also pleasant on a warm summer afternoon. Stop for fishing along the Fox River.

Nitro-powered dragsters, with plenty of accompanying fire and smoke, screech down the track at the **Great Lakes Dragway** in Union Grove (414–462–5520 or 878–3783). Broadway Bob (yep, that's his name) holds sway as owner-manager-fan-magnifico from his timing tower overlooking the rubber-scarred pavement where jet cars rock and roar. The track is in the eastern outskirts of the city, easy to find with all the signage or simply by following your ears. Parachutes often have to be used to slow down these vehicles at the end of their quarter-mile runs.

## ROCK COUNTY

Rock County is the sixth largest county in Wisconsin, located along the Illinois border. Enter the state on Interstate 90 from the Lincoln State, where there is a Wisconsin Tourist Information Center at Rest Area 22. You'll get loads of details on activities and attractions in the county and elsewhere in Wisconsin. The information building is open from 8:00 A.M. to 6:00 P.M. Monday through Saturday and from 8:00 A.M. to 4:00 P.M. Sunday from mid-May throughout October. From November to mid-May, the facility is open only from 8:00 A.M. To 4:00 P.M. Tuesday through Saturday.

The county has more than 1,500 sites listed with the National Register of Historic Places. Two towns in the northwestern part of the county are considered historic districts. The entire community of Cooksville (at the junction of Highways 138 and 59), with its splendid red brick buildings, is on the list. Most of nearby Evansville (intersection of Highways 213 and 14) is also a historical site. Ask at the tourist information center for locations and details on similarly designated sites in the vicinity.

Beloit is the first major town you'll encounter, home of the **Bartlette Memorial Historical Museum.** The museum, 2149 St. Lawrence, is on the city's west side. It's an old Victorian-era farmhouse built in the 1850s, featuring period furniture. The grounds include an old one-room schoolhouse. The museum (608–365–3811) is open from 1:00 to 4:00 P.M. daily June through August.

At ✦ **Beloit College** the ✦ **Logan Museum of Anthropology** is packed with prehistoric tools, axes and clubs, arrowheads, and other artifacts from early Indians. Beloit College, chartered in 1846, and its surrounding neighborhood are also listed as a National Register of Historic Places district. The Logan Museum (608–363–2305) is open 10:00 A.M. to 5:00 P.M., Monday through Friday, and from 11:00 A.M. to 4:00 P.M., Saturday and Sunday. Admission is free. Since the facility is on a college campus, it is closed for the usual school holidays.

For a quick picturesque drive from Beloit, drive northeast out of town on County Road X to the little crossroads communities of Shopiere and Tiffany in the Turtle Creek Valley. The latter town has a photogenic five-arch bridge over Turtle Creek. Then angle north to Janesville on either Interstate 90 or Highway 51, exiting on Highway 14 to the ✦ **Tallman Restorations,** a villa built in 1857.

The old house includes many household conveniences that were the marvels of their day. For instance, running water was supplied by an attic storage tank rather than by the typical outside pump. The place even had its own working observatory. Abraham Lincoln slept here in 1859, long after his forays in the Jefferson County Indian wars.

The Tallman House (608–752–4519) is open weekends February through May and in October. The building is open Tuesdays through Sundays, June 1 through September and is closed in January. Holiday tours from November 24 through December 31 are held Tuesday through Sunday. The first tours on the property start at 11:00 A.M., with the last one at 4:00 P.M. Tours last a bit more than an hour. Admission is charged.

North of downtown along Parker Drive is Traxler Park, where the ◆ **Rock Aqua Jays** waterskiing team demonstrates its skills at 7:00 P.M. Sunday and Wednesday nights through the summer on the Rock River. For information contact Forward Janesville, (608) 757–3160 or (800) 48PARKS.

The **Parker Pen Company,** where thousands of pens are manufactured each year, is at 1400 N. Parker Drive (608–755–7104). Free tours are offered at 1:30 P.M. from Monday through Thursday throughout the year except for the first week in July and the last week in December.

To be sure of getting on the tour, call for a reservation. The company's writing materials are used by the government for legislative bill and treaty signings and as gifts to foreign dignitaries, as well as for day-to-day use by the rest of us.

## SHEBOYGAN COUNTY

The ◆ **Kettle Moraine Vineyards,** near Highway 28 running through Cascade, is a new addition to the county's list of attractions. Don and Lani Parsons started growing hybrid grapes high in the Kettle Moraine hills in 1975 and began their winery operation in 1986. The winery is 3 miles west of Cascade on County Trunk S, one-quarter mile north of County Trunk F. After a trek through the vineyard, a sample of the wines made there is refreshing.

You may spot the likes of actor/racer Paul Newman roaming the pit area at the **Road America** track in Elkhart Lake, an hour's drive north of Milwaukee. He often comes to drive, sign autographs, and greet friends such as the Andrettis, Unsers, Sullivans, and other top drivers who always turn out for the September running of the Road America race. But don't miss the lineup of other events held on the twisting course throughout the summer, such as the Super Cycle Weekend and the Chicago Historic Races, the latter sponsored by the *Chicago Sun-Times* newspaper.

The track is one of the greatest locales for people watching in Eastern Wisconsin, as well as for watching classic race vehicles. You get there from Milwaukee by taking Interstate 43 north to where it joins Highway 57. Take 57 north to County Trunk J. Turn left (west) on J to Highway 67. Turn right (north) on 67. Road America gates are 2 miles up the highway on the left side. The grandstand near Gate 4 provides some of the best viewing, near the Corvette Corral.

A stroll along the Rotary Riverview Boardwalk on Sheboygan's Lake Michigan waterfront can be a relief from the roaring engines at Elkhart Lake. The jaunt, on South Franklin Street, goes past a historic fishing village that was once a vibrant part of the city harbor. A pleasant time for such a walk is on Sheboygan Bratwurst Day, always the first Saturday in August. Enter the eating contest: Participants see how many double brat sandwiches they can wolf down in fifteen minutes.

The **Kohler Design Center** in the village of Kohler, opened in 1985, showcases the innovative bathroom appliances built by the company that gave its name to the town. The firm is one of the world's leading manufacturers of plumbing accessories. One wall in the center is creatively stacked with red, white, black, and gray toilet bowls and bidets, framed by bathtubs, whirlpools, and similar appliances in a display called the Great Wall of China. The exhibit takes the mundane and transforms it into nifty art. Marine engines and other implements made by the company are also shown off. The center is open from 9:00 A.M. to 5:00 P.M. Tuesday through Friday and from 10:00 A.M. to 4:00 P.M. Saturday, Sunday, and holidays. Admission is free.

Kohler itself is a planned community just to the west of Sheboygan, built at the turn of the century to house plant staff. Winding streets, ivy-covered walls, and streetlights provide a charming element. The old dorm where the workers lived has been converted into a posh resort called the American Club. Prices match the elegant ambience.

## WALWORTH COUNTY

Delavan is Circus City in a state that gave birth to more than 135 shows over the past 150 years. Between 1847 and 1894, the city was winter quarters for twenty-eight of those circuses, including

P. T. Barnum's first. You'll know the town's favorite image once you pull into the downtown. A statue of a giant, rearing elephant stands on the town square.

Delavan's Spring Grove Cemetery and Old Settlers Cemetery has about one hundred famous entertainers and less-well-known workers and administrative personnel buried there. Gordon Yadon, a retired postmaster in town, offers free tours of such circus sites around town during the town's Circus Days Festival each July.

To capitalize on Delavan's colorful heritage, a group of clown fans established the ◆**Clown Hall of Fame** at 212 E. Walworth Avenue (414–728–9075), assisted by the University of Wisconsin-Extension. Regular classes on clowning, makeup, juggling, and costuming are offered at the hall of fame throughout the year. Donations of equipment and other clown gear from famous performers such as Mark Anthony and Lou Jacobs are displayed throughout the building.

A little-known spot on the 125-mile-long Kettle Moraine Drive in Jefferson County is at the intersection of Highways 12 and H, where the Bettingers operate a tiny health food store, bike repair shop, ice cream stand, bookstore, and wine shop. The **General Store** is just that, standing snug and happy in La Grange. Anita and Mike Bettinger took over an old blacksmith shop and turned it into a store with the obligatory rockers and benches on the front porch. It's just the place to come and sit awhile. Whittle if ya want.

For a fine scenic overlook of the nearby Ice Age Trail, the couple recommends starting at the **Whitewater Lake Recreation Area** ranger station, west of Walworth County Highway P on Kettle Moraine Drive. They suggest walking up the moraine on a dirt road past the gravel pit and taking the roadway about a half mile to the first open viewing area on the ridge's crest. One hundred feet below are Rice and Whitewater lakes and rolling moraines that reach to the horizon. The view is magnificent, just as the Bettingers promised.

An artesian well on Clover Valley Road, about 3 miles south of Whitewater, is popular with hikers and others who appreciate fresh, cold water. The place has been known for the past eighty or more years.

The lakes area of Walworth County, especially around Lake Geneva, is a popular resort area for Chicagoans and other Midwesterners. Fontana, Williams Bay, and Lake Geneva are small, touristy towns ringing the main lake. Larger facilities such as Lake Lawn Lodge (with several major Indian mounds on its property), Interlaken, The Abbey, and Americana Resort are well known for their spas, massages, tennis courts, horseback riding, restaurants, and meeting/convention rooms with rates to match. But who needs all that? Usually, smaller is just as good. Try the more manageable, laid-back Elizabeth Inn (414–248–9131). Only two blocks from downtown Lake Geneva, the bed and breakfast inn has an unobstructed view of the water and its own pier for swimming and fishing.

For a different sort of stay, there's the End of the Line. I don't know if you would call the place a motel or hotel because accommodations are in real cabooses (caboosi?). Each railcar has its own bathroom, beds, and the usual guest amenities. The registration lobby is called the Roundhouse and the Side Track gift shop has an assortment of railroad-themed gift items. The place is located at 301 E. Townline Road (414–248–7245).

Lake Geneva might seem a long way from Tipperary, but you can find Erin sweaters, Beleek china, and Waterford and Cavan crystal at the **Erin Isle** gift shop in the Fancy Fair Mall in downtown Lake Geneva. Owner Sarah Dann Ginko also coordinates the Grafton Street Marketplace at Milwaukee Irish Fest each August. Consequently, she knows where to find hard-to-get items of a Celtic nature. Ginko can order custom heraldic items from Ireland, as well.

Moving from Irish to Scandinavian, at least foodwise, is Scuttlebutts, at 831 Wrigley Drive (414–248–1111) on the lakefront. This family restaurant lays out the largest stacks of Swedish pancakes in town. Button's Bay Inn, 804 S. Lake Shore Drive (414–248–8336), combines a first-floor restaurant with its second-floor lodgings. Now under new management, the place was refurbished with a quaint, cozy motif. In the nearby quiet of tiny Williams Bay, Chef's Corner (414–245–6334) on Geneva Street has excellent homemade soups and German cooking. Chef's Corner is open only for dinner. The Geneva Street Grill at 10 Geneva Street in "The Bay" is another family-style restaurant, with a selection of fish, barbecue, omelets, and other tasty items at low prices. The restaurant's outside deck overlooks the lake.

For a different way to see Lake Geneva, the **Geneva Lake Cruise Line** (800–558–5911) has a hiking tour in conjunction with a spring and autumn luncheon cruise. A shoreline footpath extends all 23 miles around the lake, only 3 feet from the water.

For the hike/cruise package, park at the Riviera Boat Docks in Lake Geneva and purchase boat tickets ($22.50 for adults, $21.90 for seniors over sixty-two, and $14.55 for kids twelve and under, plus tax). You'll be walking past the Victorian-era homes of the Wrigley chewing gum heirs, the Swift meat-packing clan, and the Montgomery Ward Thorne family. The walk to Williams Bay takes about three hours to meet the luncheon cruise, for a 12:15 P.M. departure back to Lake Geneva aboard the *Belle of the Lake*.

Even with all that walking, it's an easier job than the one held by the "mailgirls" on the *Walworth II*. Working as regular summertime postal carriers, the two women leap from moving boat to dock and back again while delivering mail to homes on the lake. They have to jump to shore, run the length of a pier, drop off the mail, and leap back on the moving vessel before it gets too far away. The delivery process is a tradition that has been going on for more than seventy-five years.

Nobody has fallen into the water in recent years, but all the eager tourists on the early morning run take bets on the possibility of a damp plunge. Adults can ride the mailboat for $13.95, seniors for $12.60, students thirteen to sixteen, $11.20, and kids twelve and under, $7.25.

The two-and-one-half-hour cruise operates seven days a week between mid-June and mid-September, beginning at 9:00 A.M. from Lake Geneva Cruise Line docks. While not jumping from boat to pier, the mailgirls act as guides, describing the mansions along the shore. Call (414) 248–6206 for reservations.

## WASHINGTON COUNTY

Washington County is just north of Waukesha and Milwaukee counties, taking in the northern unit of the Kettle Moraine Forest. Follow the Kettle Moraine Drive by car or bike over landscapes carved out by glaciers 15,000 years ago. Holy Hill is the most prominent physical attraction in the county, perched high overlooking the surrounding countryside. The church looks as if it slipped off a page from a Bavarian calendar. Carmelite priests maintain a retreat center there, where you can get a great view of the forestland.

The surrounding farms and villages were first populated by Irish immigrants, including my great-grandfather and his brothers. When they emigrated from Ireland around the time of the Civil War, English agents in Canada asked them to stay there when they paused to pick up supplies. "Not on your life," swore great-grandpops Russell. "I've lived under English rule long enough," he added as a parting shot and boarded a Lake Michigan steamer bound for Milwaukee.

From Beer City, he hoofed it into the Holy Hill area, where other relatives from the Auld Sod had already settled. His experience is typical of that of many of the people still living there.

The town of Erin is a rural township with country roads named after Irish cities and provinces. Each year, the old traditions are renewed with a hilarious ◆**St. Patrick's Day parade.** The floats, horses, and marchers travel about a 3.5-mile course through the countryside beginning at the Town Hall (corner of Highways 167 and 83) and concluding at Kenealy's Erin Inn (414–673–9857) at the corner of County Trunk K and Donegal Road. To give you an idea of the "seriousness" of the event, one recent parade featured My Wild Irish Nose, a float built like a giant green schnoz, a green llama, a hillbilly band made up of grandmothers, and similar silliness. The only orange you'll ever see on parade day is the color of Washington County trucks loaded with snow fences.

The Irish cemetery at K and Emerald Drive is crowded with Whelans, Fallons, Purtells, McGraths, O'Neills, Coffeys, Mahoneys, McConvilles, Sullivans, and Hagertys. The wind sighs off the hilltops as you drive from the unfenced graveyard along Emerald, another of the state's Rustic Roads.

In eastern Washington County, on Newburg's Main Street, is the **Painted Lady,** a restaurant featuring such gourmet items as boned duck glazed with currant sauce ($12.95) and New York strip biarritz with mushrooms and shallots ($15.50). The Queen Anne–style Lady got her name from the colorful rowhouses found in San Francisco (a favorite vacation locale for the restaurant's current owner), but she had a more humble beginning as a local tavern in 1875. Since the dining room is relatively small, call (414) 675–2341 for reservations. Newburg is just inside the Washington County line on the east, along Highway 33, about 25 miles north of Milwaukee.

**117**

## WAUKESHA COUNTY

❖ **Old World Wisconsin,** operated by the Historical Society of Wisconsin, is on the map when it comes to tourist attractions. Yet its ongoing displays, programs, and activities are often over-looked. That's a shame because Old World is a great place to touch the living history of Wisconsin. More than forty buildings from around the state, originally built by immigrant settlers, have been relocated to the rolling Kettle Moraine highlands.

A motorized tram takes visitors around the 576-acre site. You can get on or off at leisure to explore the farmsites and buildings dotting the landscape. I like the museum because each commu-nity is separated from the other, to preserve the national iden-tity. Interpreters in the appropriate costumes demonstrate crafts and chores you'd find in a typical mid-nineteenth-century household. There are plenty of cows, pigs, sheep, chickens, ducks, and other critters in the pastures and pens to keep up the interest of city kids.

Seasonal events help keep the Old World feeling on the appro-priate track: spring plowing, summer planting, and autumn threshing with the era's appropriate horse-drawn equipment; Fourth of July oratory, parades, and band concerts. We've always found it fun in the winter to cross-country ski around the build-ings and over the fields. Many of the structures are open for vis-iting, even when the snow is drifting around the doorway. Each offers homemade ethnic cookies or breads, plus hot cider or hot chocolate to ward off the cold.

The museum (414–594–2116) is on Highway 67 outside the village of Eagle, about a half-hour drive south of Interstate 94.

Adjacent to the museum are the 16,600 acres of the ❖ **Southern Kettle Moraine Forest,** with a drive that tests your skill as a motorist. The ridges and valleys throughout the region were cre-ated by Ice Age glaciers. Today's roads barely tame the landscape as they loop and swirl over the ridges.

Not far from the edges of the state forest is the Genesee Depot, home of famed theatrical couple Alfred Lunt and Lynn Fontanne. Driving into the main courtyard of the sprawling complex called **Ten Chimneys** brings alive their flamboyant stage era. Lunt, who died in 1977, and Fontanne, who died in 1983, furnished their house with antiques and interesting art objects.

**Old World Wisconsin**

Drive north from Eagle on Highway 67, cross Interstate 94 on the overpass, and head into Oconomowoc. At the turn of the century, the town was a popular resort for Chicago-area business tycoons and their families who flocked to the numerous lakes dotting the vicinity. Their elegant mansions ring Lac La Belle and line the streets leading away from the water. Contemporary Oconomowoc has outgrown its quaint stage and is now a bustling community surrounded by subdivisions. The main

**119**

street, however, has several excellent galleries, antique shops, and craft stores that carry unusual items.

The **Oconomowoc Gallery & Shoppe,** 157 E. Wisconsin Avenue (414–567–8123), carries paintings, sculpture, pottery, and basketry by prominent Native American artists and craftworkers. Owners Jack and Shirley Ward made contacts with the artists while teaching at reservations. **Sun Designs,** 173 E. Wisconsin Avenue (414–567–4255), is another neat store. On display are wooden toys and models of gazebos, backyard barns, and similar structures. The company provides the plans for building your own shelter, shed, or cabana.

At 8:00 P.M. each Wednesday in June, July, and August, the Oconomowoc city band revs up a concert for the homefolks who come to the lake edge to listen. Bring your own lawn chair or blanket for a night outing. Sometimes bug spray is necessary.

I've always considered the Golden Mast Inn as having one of the best views in the state, writing about the place for *Wisconsin Trails* magazine. Owned by German restaurateurs Hans and Maria Weissgerber, the Golden Mast's dining area looks out over Okauchee Lake with its convoys of ducks and dozens of sailboats. The food matches the scenery, with loins and schnitzel as house specialties. The place (414–567–7047) is located on Lacy's Lane at Okauchee Lake, just off Highway 16 on Oconomowoc's east side. The restaurant is one of four the family owns in Waukesha County.

The ◆**Olympia Spa** to the south of Oconomowoc is well known in southeastern Wisconsin as a great place for a comfortable rejuvenation. But the place is a secret to many outsiders. Massages, steam rooms, pools, facials, exercise classes, and meals help keep visitors trim and alert. I enjoy the eucalyptus room whenever I have a head cold; the pungent steam quickly clears my head and soothes the lungs. Rates are reasonable.

The **Hawk's Inn** in nearby Delafield was built in the 1840s as a stagecoach stop. It has been refurbished as a museum, open from May through October.

County seat Waukesha has made strides to keep its downtown alive and interesting, not wanting to be caught in the all-too-often downward spiral of smaller towns. There are numerous interesting shops, including one with magician's supplies. A gazebo/bandstand, called the Silurian Springhouse, was built as a hub for the one-way streets, which zoom off in several directions. This makes it a difficult downtown for a drive-through, especially if you are unfamiliar with the area. I'd suggest you park and walk.

Waukesha means "fox" in Potawatomi, the language of one of many tribes that lived here over the generations. There are several mounds, built by earlier Native Americans, on the front lawn of the refurbished Central Library. The mounds are the only remaining ones of dozens that had been around the county prior to settlement. Most of the others have been plowed up or built over in the years since whites came into the region.

The fifty-plus mineral springs in and around Waukesha made it the center of the state's nineteenth-century spa trade. The regenerative effects of the water were supposedly discovered by Colonel Richard Dunbar, a local landowner. The good gentleman was not feeling well while out for a stroll one afternoon and took several drinks from a spring he discovered on his jaunt. Dunbar then napped under a nearby tree and allegedly woke up cured of everything that ailed him. From then on, bathhouses and health facilities sprang up, touting the wonders of Waukesha's water.

Today, only **Bethesda Roxo Waters** still bottles water for resale, as it has been doing since incorporation in 1868. The company operates out of a plant at 574 Elizabeth Street (414–547–2181), not far from Bethesda City Park on Dunbar Street. You can easily walk the few blocks there, southwest of downtown. Another natural spring is at Spring Park, near the U.S. Post Office off Broadway. Neither park currently has tap or bubbler water available, however, due to health regulations. Yet either park is comfortable for picnics—bring your own blanket, cold chicken, and fizzing bottle of Bethesda.

On the east side of town is the **Inn at Pine Terrace.** Sandy and I escaped there for a weekend getaway while writing a short piece for *Midwest Living* magazine. High on a hill overlooking Oconomowoc's lakes, the property was appropriately secluded and comfortable, with a great breakfast. The inn is located at 351 Lisbon Road (414–567–7463). It is one of several properties owned by our good friend Rip O'Dwanny, who also operates another of our favorites: the 52 Stafford Irish Inn in Plymouth (Sheboygan County).

## WAUPACA COUNTY

Waupaca is a fantastic year-round getaway for anyone who loves the outdoors. The best-known attraction is the ✦ **Chain O'Lakes,** which consist of twenty-two interlocking, spring-fed lakes which range in size from 2.5 acres to 115 acres. The waterways—packed with fish, of course—are from 8 to 100 feet deep. The first settlers arrived in the area in 1849 to establish a flour mill to serve neighboring homesteaders. In honor of the earlier Native Americans who lived in the region, the new residents selected the name Waupaca, supposedly after a local tribal leader, Wa-Puka (meaning "watching"). Historians, however, claim the name was derived from *waubeck seba,* meaning "clear water."

Regardless of whence the name, the town of Waupaca knows how to have fun. In mid-June is the Strawberry Festival, followed on July 4 with Hometown Days. A Fall-O-Rama is held the last weekend in September, with a Christmas tour of homes on the first Sunday in December. For details on events and activities, contact the Waupaca Area Chamber of Commerce, 221 S. Main Street, Box 262, Waupaca 54981 (800–236–2222 or 715–238–7343).

Waupaca is home to **Hartman Creek State Park,** which includes the Whispering Pines picnic area. Located 5 miles west of town on State Highway 54, the 1,320-acre park offers tent and RV camping (101 sites) and a group campground.

Glacial oak hills, lakes, and ponds offer a plethora of color-photo opportunities while you are hiking or biking. Call the park offices (715–258–2372) for the latest information on wildlife discussions led by naturalists. Some 5 miles of the state's thousand-mile Ice Age Trail system are also within the park boundaries. When cross-country skiing in the park, remember that the glaciers retreated from here a mere 10,000 years ago.

For a more "motorized" vacation stop in Waupaca County, Iola holds an annual Old Car Show and Swap Meet early each July. More than 2,500 show cars are displayed, with hundreds of pre-1970 vehicles up for sale. Call (715) 445–4000. Admission is charged. Iola is located at the intersection of State Highways 49 and 51. You can't miss the showgrounds—just follow the hundreds of bright posters and arrows leading to the site in the town or pull the family sedan into a procession of flashy sporters that usually putt-putt around town during the show weekend. They'll get you to the right locale.

## WINNEBAGO COUNTY

The **Bergstrom-Mahler Museum** in Neenah has more than 1,500 glass paperweights on display as part of the Evangeline Bergstrom collection. The display features handmade weights from French, English, and American manufacturers dating back one hundred years. The museum offers research facilities for other collectors by appointment from 1:00 until 4:30 P.M. on Wednesday and Thursday. The library is filled with material, and there is a workroom in which to look over samples and talk with curators. The museum is located at 165 N. Park Avenue, Neenah 54956 (414–729–4658).

The Doty Cabin on Webster and Lincoln in Neenah is a replica of the home of Wisconsin's second territorial governor, James Duane Doty. The building houses numerous pioneer artifacts, including many of the governor's own possessions. The cabin is open from 1:00 to 5:00 P.M. from mid-June to mid-August. Call the Neenah Parks and Recreation Department, (414) 751–4614, for more information. Admission is free.

Oshkosh, home of the OshKosh B'Gosh jeans, is also home of the world's largest fly-in event: the ◆**Experimental Aircraft Association (EAA) Fly-in** held each August at Wittman Field. Warbirds, mini-aircraft, gliders, and regular private planes jam the fields surrounding the airport. The EAA aviation center museum is located at 3000 Poberezny Drive (414–426–4800), with hundreds of aircraft and accessories on display.

From Oshkosh, drive northwest on State Highway 110 to tiny Zittau, where some of the best cheese curds in Wisconsin can be found at the Union Star Cheese Factory (414–836–2804). Non-Wisconsinites always wonder about the lumpy-looking curds, which make a delightfully squeaky sound when chewed. The curds are especially good with smoked catfish, crisp rye crackers, and freshly squeezed lemonade or a just-tapped beer.

# MILWAUKEE AND ENVIRONS

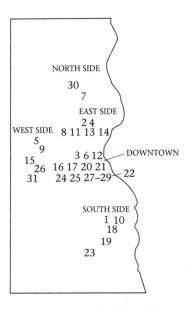

NORTH SIDE
30
7

EAST SIDE
2 4
WEST SIDE  8 11 13 14
5
9            3 6 12 — DOWNTOWN
15
26  16 17 20 21
31    24 25 27–29  22

SOUTH SIDE
1 10
18
19
23

1. Haupt Barrel and Cooperage
   Company
2. Napoleon's
3. Eccola's Direct European
   Imports
4. Art Smart's Dart Mart and
   Juggling Emporium
5. Femzac African International
   Imports
6. Usinger's
7. African Center
8. Woodland Pattern
9. Kehr's Kandy Kitchen
10. Goldmann's Department
    Store
11. High Wind Bookstore
12. Harry W. Schwartz Book
    Shop
13. Coffee Trader
14. Sendik's

15. Miller Bakery
16. Polaris Restaurant
17. Sheila's Cafe at the Plaza
18. Nash's Irish Castle
19. Zur Krone
20. Boobie's Place
21. Dean Jensen's Gallery
22. Piano Gallery
23. Pinewood Galleries
24. Michael Lord Gallery
25. Lakefront Festival of the
    Arts
26. Miller Brewing Co.
27. Pabst Brewing Co.
28. Sprecher Brewing Co.
29. Water Street Brewery
30. Havenwoods Environmental
    Awareness Center
31. Sherman Park Blues and
    Family Fest

# MILWAUKEE AND ENVIRONS

The Potawatomi Indians called Milwaukee the "Gathering Place by the Waters," indicating a neutral ground. Tribes from around the Midwest could relax on the shaded banks of the Milwaukee and Menomonee rivers and compare notes on buffalo hunting, just as today's conventioneers do about sales figures. Wild rice was thick in the swamps, and a large bluff separated the river valley from Lake Michigan. The hard, sandy beach was perfect for racing horses.

Of course, that was all before the first European settlers moved into the region. The explorer-priest Father Jacques Marquette pulled his canoe up on the riverbank in 1674 (a site now called Pere Marquette Park, located behind the Milwaukee County Historical Society, 910 N. Old World Third Street, 414–273–8288). He was followed later by French trappers, who in turn were followed by Yankee land speculators. Next came the settlers. Soon the swamps were gone, the bluff was covered with houses, and the beach was a lakefront park.

Yet Milwaukee still retains that gathering-place image, proud of the potpourri of heritages that make up the roster of residents. Any visitor to the city finds that out immediately. Ethnic festivals, parades, church events, lectures, exhibitions, folk fairs, and a host of other events celebrate Milwaukee's dozens of nationalities. And it's a city of neighborhoods. Sherman Park, Merrill Park, Bay View, Walker's Point, Harambee, and the others have their different housing and lifestyle flavors. About 610,000 persons live in the city, making it the largest in the state. Including the entire metro area doubles that figure.

You should start a jaunt at the Greater Milwaukee Convention and Visitors Bureau, 510 W. Kilbourn Avenue 53203 (414–273–3950), for the latest in brochures and information on attractions and events. Another visitor information center is located at General Mitchell Field, 5300 S. Howell Avenue (414–747–4808). For weekend updates on events, call the city's Funline of Events (414–799–1177). The Milwaukee County Transit System (414–937–3252) has summer tours around the city, with pickups at the major downtown hotels. The trip ($10 for adults, $8.00 for seniors and kids under twelve) beats driving and provides a good orientation for first-time visitors.

From here, you should be able to strike out to see the city, currently going through a downtown building boom that includes a new major-league auditorium, a theater district, office towers, and hotels. Visitors who haven't been to Milwaukee in several years often find themselves turned around because the old landmarks have given way to the new.

You don't have to hit the shopping malls for interesting rummaging. There are favorite places where a shopper can count on excellent service, ease in access, unique items, and knowledgeable clerks. To find your way around the world, there's the **Milwaukee Map Service,** 959 N. Mayfair Road (414–774–1300 or –800–525–3822). The place is a magnet for geography buffs. Just the thing for *Off the Beaten Path* readers is the series of Wisconsin regional maps that show every road in the state. Each section costs $5.00. The map store is open from 8:00 A.M. to 5:00 P.M. Monday through Friday and from 9:00 A.M. to 4:00 P.M. Saturday.

Now that you know your way around, head for Milwaukee's South Side and take in the ◆**Haupt Barrel and Cooperage Company,** 1432 S. First Street (414–645–7274). The company was founded in 1917 and still sells barrels and casks for commercial customers. The firm went into the wine barrel business about a decade ago. Owner Gene Haupt can show off a press, talk about grapes, and give suggestions on which Ozark-crafted keg is best for wine storage.

Up the street from Haupt's is the **Forelle Fish Netting Corporation,** which sells netting for soccer goals, fishing, and even curtains. Its customers include the Milwaukee County Zoo, commercial fishers, and interior decorators. The quiet little store is located at 1030 S. First Street (414–672–5935).

At the other end of town, in the suburb of Shorewood, is ◆**Napoleon's,** 3948 N. Maryland Avenue (414–962–6730). The store is crammed with war games, models, lead figurines, and accessories for the Dungeons & Dragons set. Owner Fritz von Buchholtz has opened a large basement for game players who utilize a wall-to-wall table for their imaginary conquests via tiny soldiers. This shop is son Dan's most favorite store in ten states. One of mine, too . . .

◆**Eccola's Direct European Imports** is in a dangerous place. At 237 N. Broadway, it's just two blocks from my office on N. Water Street. Eccola's is a browser's paradise, where you can spend a few minutes or an hour perusing the plaster artworks, wood carvings, furniture, and similar eclectic items.

While Eccola's is too close for comfort on most days when I should be working rather than roaming, it can't be beat when birthday or Christmas gift-buying time rolls around.

Whenever we think we have too many balls in the air, when the job seems overwhelming, when things start falling out of the sky, a quick fix comes at ◆ **Art Smart's Dart Mart and Juggling Emporium,** 1695 N. Humboldt Street (414–273–DART). There's a psychological boost gained just by walking through the front door and knowing that many customers here drop a lot of things while perfecting their techniques. Glass cases are packed with Indian clubs, torches, beanbags, balls, and other similar tools. Hanging on the walls are darts, dart boards, wind-up airplanes, and a host of other geegaws. And kites! There are dragons, birds, and jets . . . red kites, yellow kites, blue kites, and rainbow kites. You can't beat it.

◆ **Femzac African International Imports,** 4405 N. 60th Street (414–536–8255), has a colorful selection of clothing, printed cloth, jewelry, and other artifacts. The shop is one of the larger such retailers in the Midwest, and the motto is, "if they don't have it, they'll try to find a way to get it."

If you are into sausage in the wurst way, ◆ **Usinger's** in downtown Milwaukee (1030 Old World Third Street, 414–276–9100) has pounds and pounds of the stuff made the good, old-fashioned German way. Many of the clerks speak with a hint of a home country accent. Hungry crowds pack the company's showroom on Saturday mornings for their weekly purchases, so go midweek if you can to avoid the rush.

The ◆ **African Center** import and food store (1912 W. Hampton Avenue, 414–263–6153) serves the growing black Caribbean community in Milwaukee, as well as city residents originally from Kenya, Nigeria, Malawi, and other African nations. Vincent Awosika and his brother, Charles, have regularly sponsored fashion shows, featuring bright, contemporary designs from those regions.

◆ **Woodland Pattern** (720 E. Locust Street, 414–263–5001) presents an extensive selection of small press and poetry books, feminist literature, Third World kids' stories, and New Age albums. A large hall doubles as an art/photo gallery, as well as a stage for a regularly scheduled calendar of poetry readers and musicians.

Easter means chocolate eggs, jelly beans, and fairy food at ❖**Kehr's Kandy Kitchen** (3533 W. Lisbon Avenue, 414–344–4305). The weeks before the holiday, the tiny white building overflows with folks hunting for the perfect nest-filler for their kids, grandchildren . . . or themselves. Bill Kehr makes all his goodies. Chocolate-covered cherries, white almond chocolate . . . ah, that list is tempting. Bill is also an accomplished polka organist, lining his walls with albums for sale.

For anyone with a love of things British, **Bits of Britain** (1201 E. Russell Avenue, 414–744–3989) has tins of biscuits, homemade scones, jams, cheeses, portraits of the royal family, appropriate flags, and gift items. Three little tables in a back room are just the right size for teatime. A delicate lace doily hangs from the window, creating a soft shadow on the red tablecloths. A painting of the queen smiles down on folks who have discovered this quaint corner of the old empire. Bits of Britain is a snug little place where meat pies, mushy peas with vinegar, and cakes go over well. You can peek around the corner and watch everything being prepared in the open kitchen. Christmastime is the best season, when plum puddings are stacked like the crown jewels, and the clerks often slip a lolly or gummy bear to visiting youngsters. Bits of Britain also has a shop at 294 W. Main Street in Waukesha.

There are several streets on which you'll find a number of specialty stores, eateries, and entertainment outlets that are must-visits.

Mitchell Street on the South Side has been tagged bridal row because of the numerous wedding shops there. You can get anything you've ever dreamed of in ❖**Goldmann's Department Store,** 930 W. Mitchell Street (414–645–9100). The firm has been a neighborhood staple there for generations. Wringer washing machines, corsets, and oversized jeans (large enough to hold three regular-weight men) are included in the stock.

The lunch counter is the best in town for people watching and listening for Milwaukeese, the jargon of the city that warrants a chuckle. "Let's go down by Schuster's where the streetcar bends the corner around" is one of the most famous examples.

The trendy East Side of the city near the University of Wisconsin–Milwaukee has ❖**High Wind Bookstore** for the latest in alternative publications, metaphysical essays, New Age literature, and soothing instrumental mood music. The cozy shop, with its incense and candles providing a relaxing ambience, is located at 3041 N. Oakland Avenue, (414) 332–8288.

Take in a ✦**Harry W. Schwartz Book Shop** in Milwaukee if you need extra copies of *Wisconsin: Off the Beaten Path*. There's one in suburban Brookfield, another on Oakland Avenue, and the flagship in the Iron Block Building at the corner of Wisconsin Avenue and Water Street. This historic turn-of-the-century building has a facade actually made of iron. Ah, it's for really "heavy" readers. Excuse me . . .

Everybody who is anybody stops by ✦**Coffee Trader** (2625 N. Downer Avenue, 414–332–9690), the place to see and be seen in the trendy neighborhood not far from the University of Wisconsin–Milwaukee. Whenever possible, I like to hang out by the sun-warmed front windows, down a pot of tea, and read the morning paper. The Trader is great for after-theater stops for cheesecake, Bass ale, or freshly ground Kenyan coffee.

✦**Sendik's** (2643 N. Downer Avenue, 414–962–1600) is one of the largest fresh fruit and vegetable stores in the city. Ready-made bouquets are conveniently located by the front door, for shoppers and lovers in a hurry. Tony Sendik also runs a fresh fish shop in his store, where you can get hot carryouts of fish and chips.

In the 4600 and 4700 blocks of Burleigh Street on the near West Side, several kosher stores sell lox, bagels, and all the trimmings for a hearty breakfast. Since 1923, ✦**Miller Bakery** (4715 W. Burleigh Street, 414–445–8814) has made the tops in heavy rye breads. I especially like the pumpernickel, served with fresh liverwurst and raw onion.

The neighborhood around the intersection of West Lisbon and West North avenues, where they connect diagonally, has an intercontinental flair, with an Indian grocery, two Greek and several Oriental restaurants, a Greek gift shop, a Black Muslim mosque, and a Chicago-style hot dog stand.

Milwaukeeans, like the army, travel on their stomachs. There must be more high-quality eating places in this city than almost anywhere else. The best skyline view is from the ✦**Polaris Restaurant** atop the Hyatt Regency Hotel (333 W. Kilbourn, 414–276–1234). You can whiz to the top of the hotel aboard one of those glass-enclosed elevators with the twinkling lights. This is an occasion eatery, for birthdays, anniversaries, special tête-à-têtes. The room rotates a full turn every forty-five minutes, to give you a look at the City Hall, the downtown construction, the lake, and the roadways leading into the city. There's nothing like it while dining on a lobster tail and sipping a rare vintage. Prices range from moderate to expensive.

❖**Sheila's Cafe at the Plaza** in the old art deco Plaza is a step back into the mid-1930s. Autographed photos of Clark Gable, film posters, and other memorabilia are tastefully positioned so they aren't overwhelming but lend a gracious look to the small cafe. In the summer, a backyard patio is opened for casual breakfasts and lunch (no dinners served here), with classical music softly playing in the background. The owner started her career with a hot dog cart on Wisconsin Avenue and eventually graduated to this upscale hideaway, one that you wouldn't notice unless you knew it was there. The hotel itself belongs on some Hollywood movie set. Look closely at the corner of Cass and State streets and Sheila's appears. If lost, call (414) 272–4661.

What would Milwaukee be without its pubs? Some neighborhoods have a bar on each corner, plus an extra one in the middle, all of which have their regular clientele. Water Street downtown near City Hall now has a "strip" of bars and restaurants that attract the upwardly mobile set. But here are some special ones where neckties are certainly unnecessary and a down-home feel without pretension is prevalent.

❖**Nash's Irish Castle** (1328 W. Lincoln Avenue, 414–643–9654) has ceili (kay-lee) dancing every Wednesday night. It's also the regular meeting place for a number of Irish organizations. You don't even need to talk with an Irish accent. The place is run by Josie and Kit Nash, both formerly of Dublin. Kit was the 1988 Irishman of the Year for the Shamrock Club of Wisconsin's Milwaukee chapter.

❖**Zur Krone** (839 S. Second Street, 414–647–1910) is a typical German-style Milwaukee bar, with paintings of assorted emperors and kings adorning the wall above the back bar. There's also a drawing of comic strip character Bill the Cat for a light touch. Zur Krone has more than 200 international beers on stock for sampling. You can even join a club, winning a glass drinking boot and a lot of adulation after sampling a certain number of brews. The tavern is open for lunch, serving homemade soups and chili in addition to hearty sandwiches on bread and buns made by a nearby Mexican bakery. We've often stopped here on rainy or wintry Saturdays after touring the Milwaukee harbor a few blocks to the east. While the kids played checkers or chess with the boards provided by the establishment, I catch up on the latest gossip.

For long, drawn-out blues that just don't seem to quit, ❖ **Boobie's Place** is the place to be. You can order great catfish and greens early in the evening, but the best food is for the musical soul as night rolls around. Free blues are laid on the table five nights a week. On Tuesdays musicians bring their own gear to jam. Boobie's is located at 502 W. Garfield Place (414–263–3399). It's open seven days a week from 10:30 A.M. to 2:00 A.M. Boobie is actually Everett Moore, who runs the joint with his family. He's usually holding court behind the bar.

Food for the cultural soul can be had at the small galleries dotting the Milwaukee landscape. ❖ **Dean Jensen's Gallery** (165 N. Broadway, 414–278–7100) was opened by the former art critic for the *Milwaukee Sentinel* newspaper. The ❖ **Piano Gallery** (219 N. Milwaukee Street, 414–276–3525) shows its works in a studio where concert pianos are tuned and refurbished. Wildlife art specialists are featured in the ❖ **Pinewood Galleries** (9724 W. Forest Home Avenue, 414–529–3638). The ❖ **Michael Lord Gallery** is in the Pfister Hotel (424 E. Wisconsin Avenue, 414–273–8222).

Augmenting the gallery scene are the dozens of art fairs around the community, ranging from the nationally renowned ❖ **Lakefront Festival of the Arts** in June on the grounds of the lakefront Milwaukee Art Center to neighborhood and college fairs. The weather is usually cold and rainy for at least one day out of the three for the lakefront fest. Keep an umbrella handy, just in case.

The city has several nicknames, with "Beer City" probably the most well known. ❖ **Miller Brewing Co.** (3950 W. Highland Avenue, 414–931–2337) and ❖ **Pabst Brewing Co.** (915 W. Juneau Avenue, 414–223–3709) are the only two major breweries now operating. Each offers tours, followed by a stop in their sampling rooms.

The old Jos. Schlitz brewery buildings are being converted into condos and office space. But brewing is certainly not dying in Milwaukee. Several years ago, microbrewery ❖ **Sprecher Brewing Co.** (730 W. Oregon Street, 414–272–2337) started operations and has found a definite market niche between the giants.

**Miller Brewing Co.**

The ◆ **Water Street Brewery** (1101 N. Water Street, 414–272–1195) opened late in 1987, serving its own house beer made on the premises. The process is completed in vats in the bar's front windows, resulting in Water Street Amber, Old World Oktoberfest, and Sporten European Lager, as well as seasonal beers.

Milwaukee is also known as Cream City, a legacy of the nineteenth century when many homes were constructed from a creamy colored brick. The houses are easily spotted around town, with large concentrations in the older neighborhoods on the near South Side and along the lakefront. For a time, more workers labored in the brickyards than in the breweries, producing 40,000 million bricks a year. For a peek at how the other half lives, take a jaunt along Lake Shore Drive (Highway 32 of Red Arrow Division fame) past Milwaukee's Gold Coast mansions. Some are of the distinctive Cream City brick.

Even with the dense population, pockets of calm are easily found in a city that cherishes its parks and open spaces. ◆ **Havenwoods Environmental Awareness Center** (6141 N. Hopkins Street, 414–527–0232) has a 240-acre tract of fields and woodlots with 3 miles of marked trails. The center is a twenty-minute drive from the Central City. Many school programs utilize the site for nature study programs. Another getaway is the lakefront bike trail that wanders north from near the Henry W. Maier Lakefront Festival Park into the suburbs. The roadway is located on an abandoned railroad right-of-way, so the pedaling is smooth and easy. The three climate-controlled domes of the **Mitchell Park Horticultural Conservatory** (524 S. Layton Avenue, 414–649–9800) are well-known Milwaukee landmarks. Their floral displays, rain forest, and desert area are always worth a stop. **Boerner Botanical Garden** in Whitnall Park (5879 S. 92nd Street, 414–425–1130) is another site where the bloom is always on the rose.

The Department of City Development has come up with a nifty promotion for a number of its neighborhoods. Called MKE Neighborhood Tours Ltd., the plan features a walking-driving itinerary, similar to what would be prepared by a travel agency. The information tells everything you need to know about an area, from historical cemeteries to local eateries. All stops are numbered on a readable map. Take in the "Mitchell Street Express," "Neighborhoods North and All That Jazz," "Bayview," "Riverwest," and "I–94 West." For individual tour packets, contact the DCD, 809 N.

Broadway, Box 324, Milwaukee 53201. This is one of the easiest ways to really get off the beaten path in the city.

The Department of City Development has also devised several historic building tours around Milwaukee, taking in the Bay View, Juneautown, Kilbourntown, North Point, Walker's Point, and West End neighborhoods. Flyers on each area include maps and point-by-point descriptions of famous old structures found along the way. Combine one of these jaunts with the MKE Neighborhood program, and you will really learn the face of the city. Be ready to stop in at any of the mom-and-pop groceries and restaurants found along the way. Copies of the flyers can also be secured from DCD.

Milwaukee is noted as The City of Festivals, with a delightful menu of ethnic activities on the lakefront through the Great Circus Parade, which brings colorful wagons to the city from the Circus World Museum in Baraboo each July. But there are off-the-beaten-path events that should not be missed, ranging from Greek and Serbian festivals to church fairs. One of the best events off the main street is the ◆**Sherman Park Blues and Family Fest,** held at the end of July. "Shermfest," as it is affectionately called, draws in music lovers of all ages from throughout the community for a real reunion-type affair, set to the strains of The Old Blues Boys, Big Bob and the Ballroom Blitz, the Jim Liban Combo, the Blues Disciples, and dozens of other groups. The Sherman Park neighborhood, where we once lived, is a racially mixed area of beautiful homes and wide boulevards. The park itself is tucked into a corner of West Burleigh Street and Sherman Avenue on the city's near West Side.

Milwaukee is an easy city in which to drive, even with the seemingly endless construction. Laid out by straight-thinking German engineers, most roads run east to the lake or due north and south. Seldom does an out-of-town driver get lost, except possibly while trying to find an on-ramp to Interstate 94. If you spend too much time spinning around blocks, ask a patrol officer (yes, Milwaukee still has beat cops) or hole up in a Milwaukee hotel.

Lodgings range from the grande dames of Milwaukee's accommodations world at the Pfister Hotel (424 E. Wisconsin Avenue, 414–273–8222) and her sister, the Marc Plaza (509 W. Wisconsin Avenue, 414–271–7250), to the usual collection of chain motels.

The Pfister, a Triple-A four-diamond award winner and member of Preferred Hotels and Resorts Worldwide, was named Hotel of the Year in 1991 by the Wisconsin Innkeepers Association. The venerable hotel celebrated its one hundredth anniversary in 1993.

For bed and breakfast listings, contact Bed and Breakfast of Milwaukee, 320 E. Buffalo Street 53202 (414–271–BEDS). Prices range from $25 to $100 a night. For reservations, contact Barbara Gardner, who lists an average of twenty-three homes seasonally. Summer weekends are always the busiest, especially around ethnic festival dates.

You'll need such a rest stop after galloping around town.

# Appendix: How to Obtain Additional Information

Wisconsin has five year-round and three seasonal information centers at its borders with Illinois, Iowa, and Minnesota. You may wish to pull into any one of them for a driving break and to browse through the brochure racks, check on maps, and discover what's going on in nearby communities. Bathrooms are readily accessible.

Open all year are facilities at Beloit (Rest Area 96, Interstate 90); Hudson (Rest Area 25, Interstate 94); Kenosha (Rest Area 26, Interstate 94); La Crosse (Rest Area 31, Interstate 90); and Madison (123 Washington Street).

Open mid-May through October are Genoa City (Rest Area 24, Highway 12); Prairie du Chien (at the Highway 18 bridge); and Superior (Rest Area 23, Highways 2 and 53).

For the convenience of travelers, the state has 32 year-round, heated toilet stops along major highways and 163 primitive sites. The latter are closed in off-season, so plan to accommodate your carload of kids accordingly. Look for the red triangle on state road maps for locations.

Aside from being functional, most of the sites offer the bonus of exceptional views of the countryside. One of the best, for instance, is about 5 miles west of Fennimore on Highway 18. On both sides of the road, deep valleys roll toward the horizon. Currier & Ives farmsites dot the oak-shrouded hills, their red barns and white houses dappling the scenery. A tired traveler can lie on a sun-drenched summer hillside there and count clouds before meandering eastward toward Madison or west toward the Mississippi River. Unfortunately, the bathrooms are among those locked in the winter, although the access road is plowed. I've always wanted to stop and go sledding there on our holiday trips to see Iowa relatives, but for one reason or another, we've always had to forgo the thrill of swooshing down the steep hillsides.

Historical sites abound in Wisconsin. There's the usual selection of baronial mansions, rough-hewn pioneer settlements, and George-Washington-slept-here-sort-of-places—not that the famous Founding Father ever actually visited Wisconsin according to anyone's tall tale, but many other presidents and other notables have dropped by since then, either simply to say hello or to do some fishing.

Don't whiz past the numerous historical markers scattered along Wisconsin's highways. Nobody has ever kept an accurate total of the state, county, and local signposts, but 3,000 is a conservative estimate. They'll tell you of famous personalities, famous fires, famous floods, famous Indian battles, and famous industries. Roadway signs about a half mile before each marker alert motorists that such a monument is just down the pike.

One prime way to wander Wisconsin is to follow any of the fifty officially designated paved or gravel Rustic Roads at key points about the state. The program started in 1973, with the first designation made in 1975. The roadways range from 2.5 to 10 miles long. They are marked by easily identifiable brown-and-yellow signs and highlighted by an outline of the state's boundaries to indicate the appropriate routes. For a free map and brochure telling about these "less traveled roads," write to the Rustic Roads Board, Wisconsin Department of Transportation, Box 7913, Madison 53707 (608–266–0639).

To have one of its byways so designated, a community or county submits an application to the board, which reviews the proposal and looks to see if it fits the following criteria: The road should have outstanding natural attributes such as native vegetation, scenic vistas, or historical significance; it should be lightly traveled; no scheduled widening or other improvement can be scheduled to detract from the original condition of the road upon application; and the road should be at least 2 miles long.

For the latest general information on the state's travel scene, contact the **Wisconsin Division of Tourism,** Department of Development, 123 W. Washington Avenue, Box 7970, Madison 53707 (608–266–7621, 800–ESCAPES, or 800–432–TRIP).

The state's primary tourism regions will provide details about a specific area, so write or call:

Milwaukee and environs, **Greater Milwaukee Convention and Visitors Bureau,** 510 W. Kilbourn Street, Milwaukee 53203 (414–273–7222).

**Hidden Valleys,** 6711 Settlement Road, Cassville 53806 (608–725–5867).

**Indian Head Country,** Box 628, Chetek 54728 (715–924–2970 or 800–472–6654 in Wisconsin).

**Northern Initiative,** Box 217, Cable 54821 (800–533–7454).
**Southeastern Wisconsin Tourism Federation,** 818 E.
Brown Street, Waupun 53963 (414–324–4431).

For information about specific lodgings, attractions, or parks,
contact the following:

**State Historical Society of Wisconsin,** 816 State Street,
Madison 53706 (608–264–6400).

**Wisconsin Association of Campground Owners
(WACO),** Box 1770, Eau Claire 54702 (715–839–9226). To
receive a mailed directory of the 149 WACO members, send the
organization $2.00 to cover postage. Otherwise, they are free at
tourist information centers, travel shows, chambers of commerce,
and campgrounds.

**Wisconsin Department of Natural Resources,** Bureau of
Parks & Recreation, Box 7921, Madison 53707 (608–266–2181).

**Wisconsin Innkeepers Association,** 509 W. Wisconsin
Avenue, Milwaukee 53203 (414–271–2851).

**Wisconsin Restaurant Association,** 31 S. Henry Street,
Suite 300, Madison 53703 (608–251–3663).

**Bed & Breakfast Guide,** c/o Carol J. Buelow, Box 566, Madison 53705 (608–238–3663). Send $7.95 for a ninety-six page-
guide with 145 listings; no reservation service.

**Wisconsin Youth Hostels,** c/o American Youth Hostels,
2224 W. Wisconsin Avenue, Milwaukee 53233 (414–933–1170).
Office hours are from 5:00 to 7:00 P.M. Monday and 9:00 A.M. to
1:00 P.M. Tuesday through Friday.

Remember that most communities have a chamber of commerce or tourist office eager to help with drop-in requests.
They'll load you down with printed material or describe the
best place in town for pecan pie. Or simply stop in at the corner
pub, ask at the local gas station, or inquire of a passerby. Most
likely, you'll get some friendly suggestions and lots of advice on
what to see and do locally.

For a monthly look at what Wisconsin has to offer, especially
in the nooks and crannies of the state, subscribe to *Wisconsin
Trails,* 6225 University Avenue, Box 5650, Madison 53705
(608–231–2444). The glossy, comprehensive magazine is published bimonthly ($19.95 a year or $3.95 per issue). Articles range
from folksy pieces on how to bake onion-dill bread to reports on
the latest bed and breakfast facility. I've written features for the

magazine on subjects such as kringle bakers in Racine or Milwau-kee's best ethnic eateries. My subsequent paunch proclaims proudly that "somebody has to do it."

For a selection of excellent maps of the state, secure a copy of the *Wisconsin Atlas & Gazetteer* ($12.95) by the DeLorme Mapping Company, Box 298, Freeport, ME 04032 (207–865–4171). The state is broken into eighty-one quadrangular topographical sections, which show every bump and nonbeaten path in the Badger State. There's also listings of bike routes, canoe trips, lighthouses, waterfalls, and a ton of other handy information for anyone into hard-core meandering.

So, as you can tell, there's a lot of help available for planning an off-the-beaten-path expedition. In fact, the latest tourism department motto is "You're Among Friends" in Wisconsin. Take them for their word. After all, any state that hosts the U.S. Water-melon Seed Spitting Championships has to have a lot of affable neighborliness going for it.

# General Index

# INNS

# MUSEUMS

## STATE, COUNTY, AND LOCAL PARKS

## ABOUT THE AUTHORS

Martin Hintz is an award-winning travel writer from the Milwaukee area who has been writing about the Midwest for almost twenty years. His articles have appeared in dozens of national and regional magazines and newspapers. He has also written geographies for young people, covering Midwestern states as well as European, Latin American, and African countries. Hintz belongs to the Midwest Travel Writers Association and the Society of American Travel Writers, among other professional journalism groups. Co-author Dan is now in college, majoring in film. He has lived in Russia and Venezuela and traveled throughout England and Scotland.

Dan's sister, Kate, helped a great deal with this third edition of *Wisconsin* by double-checking facts and phone numbers. Brother Steve had assisted with the second edition. All three Hintz kids have traveled extensively with their parents.